ELY

ELY

An Autobiography

by ELY GREEN

Foreword by BERTRAM WYATT-BROWN
Introduction by LILLIAN SMITH
Afterword by ARTHUR BEN CHITTY

Brown Thrasher Books
The University of Georgia Press
Athens and London

Published in 1990 as a Brown Thrasher Book
by the University of Georgia Press
Athens, Georgia 30602

Ely: An Autobiography © 1966 by the Seabury Press,
   Incorporated
Introduction © 1966 by Lillian Smith
Foreword © 1990 by the University of Georgia Press
Afterword © 1990 by Arthur Ben Chitty

The paper in this book meets the guidelines for permanence
and durability of the Committee on Production Guidelines for
Book Longevity of the Council on Library Resources.

Printed in the United States of America

94 93 92 91 90   5 4 3 2 1

Library of Congress Cataloging in Publication Data

Green, Ely, 1893–
    Ely : an autobiography / by Ely Green ; foreword by
    Bertram Wyatt-Brown, introduction by Lillian Smith ;
    afterword by Arthur Ben Chitty.
    p. cm.
    Reprint, with new introd. Originally published: New York :
    Seabury Press © 1966.
    "Brown thrasher books."
    ISBN 0-8203-2397-7
    1. Green, Ely, 1893–   . 2. Afro-Americans—Biography.
3. Mulattoes—United States—Biography.   4. Sewanee
    (Tenn.)—Biography.   I. Title.
    E185.97.G795A3   1990
    305.8'9607302—dc20
[B]   90-10704
                                                CIP

Foreword

In a memorable essay some years ago, C. Vann Woodward argued that the South's most distinguishing feature in a nation of almost uniform progress was its tragic history. In contrast to the easy optimism and material growth of the North, the southern states had experienced the calamities of unredeemed defeat in blood-drenched war, penury, and racial intolerance. Since the rest of mankind has been similarly beleaguered, the North, the distinguished historian asserted, was the region out of step, an irony too long overlooked in perilous self-celebration.[1]

Irony may also be found in so small a microcosm as the village of Sewanee, Tennessee, a ten-thousand-acre forested retreat of learning for the southern Episcopal church. There Ely Green, born in 1893, grew to young manhood. We associate the University of the South, the town's only *raison d'être*, with its processions of bishops in billowing robes and undergraduates in black gowns, its gabled Victorian houses and Oxfordian spires of local sandstone—and its organ of southern culture, the *Sewanee Review*. From its founding the year before Ely Green was born to the present day, that quarterly has served as a major intellectual enterprise for established and aspiring poets, short-story writers, and literary critics. William P. Trent, Allen Tate, Robert Penn Warren, Donald Davidson, Andrew Lytle, Caroline Gordon, John Crowe Ransom, Monroe Spears, and other luminaries have edited or faithfully contributed to its pages. As an awestruck sophomore at the college, I remember watching the English poet Stephen Spender and "Red" Warren play croquet on the lawn in front of Tuckaway Inn as the afternoon sun gleamed through the oaks. Later, the croquet-players and John Palmer, then editor of the *Review*, half seriously cooked up literary controversies to boost circulation as they drank tea and ate powdered raisin biscuits, customary teatime fare at "Bairnwick." So named in the English-manor mode like many other southern houses, Bairnwick was the spacious home of the Reverend George Boggan Myers, with his gates-ajar collar and gentle Mississippi manners. In dignity and intellect the seminary dean was not unique among the faculty members, but in conduct and appearance he echoed an earlier era during which Ely Green's story takes place.

This was the Sewanee most everyone whoever heard of it knows best: "a place," said Will Percy in *Lanterns on the Levee*, "to be hopelessly sentimental about." With its informal constabulary of "old ladies who were always old and ladies and who never die" (to borrow again from Percy), Sewanee, particularly in his and Ely Green's day, had been only as elegant as the limited resources of professors, chaplains, and descendants of once-wealthy Confederate generals could manage to make it.[2] Except for some persistent Kirby-Smiths, the other generals' heirs have long since gone away. Retired veterans of more recent conflicts have taken

vi

their place. The "inmates," as Percy once called them, and even the faculty, now enjoy the plenitude of current southern prosperity. At an earlier time, however, the students had imported a certain air of impoverished Episcopal gentility when at each beginning of term they disembarked from the "Mountain Goat." Once daily, the train came up the western slope from the shabby, valley junction at Cowan. Its tracks were to be the means for Ely Green's hasty departure.

This black man's story is about that turn-of-the century era when the manners, prejudices, and rituals of an Old South ambience still lingered. But it concerns a metaphorically and literally darker side of regional life. Even the most benign and well-meaning white Christian appears to us in a different age as either blind or consciously hypocritical. Such a latter-day assessment is easy to make. At that juncture in southern history, however, the only source of protection—as the confrontation between Ely's sister Ann and the cove-dweller Perry demonstrates—was a gentleman like the knightly Mr. Rosborough. The patriarchal order also served as the sole means of patronage for a young and ambitious black, flawed, evasive, faithless or impotent against the forces of a cruel populist racism though it often was. Indeed, for a while the white apostles of the paternal code found a place for Ely Green. But, as he grew from child to man, he became increasingly an embarrassment and an anomaly. Those high ideals of an honorable bearing could not accommodate the inquiring mind and vigorous soul of young Ely Green and the feelings of malice and jealousy that he aroused. The system failed him and itself.

How strange and yet how fitting that he should become the spokesman for a silent, anonymous population. His people cooked the meals, swept the corridors, and tended the lawns of this lonely, unspoiled outpost of gentle cultivation amidst the Tennessee hills not far from the Alabama border. Ely Green was never destined, however, to be a figure in the "southern (white) literary renaissance." Years after he had left Sewanee, that outpouring of creativity helped to make famous the august *Review*. Green was more likely to serve than drink China tea, to groom sleek thoroughbreds than ride them, to seek advice, hat in hand, than grandly dispense it.

Nonetheless, despite the outward simplicity of his recollections, the autobiography is as classically southern as the works of Warren, Tate, Ransom, and Lytle. "Southern" should never be defined in white terms alone. We should remember such black exiles as Ralph Ellison, Jean Toomer, Richard Wright, and Zora Neale Hurston, among others. Quite clearly, Green owes his astonishing gift of storytelling primarily to his black heritage, though white oral traditions had been equally influential in the creation of the celebrated regional literature. Moreover, with candid fidelity he records conversations of defiance and resentment among the blacks in Sewanee and in Bridgeport, Alabama. In the latter place he was quickly introduced to the religion and the mores of his kinspeople, a necessary part of his development, as he recognized himself.

One is reminded first of Ned Cobb, another shrewd black storyteller. Theodore Rosengarten memorialized him in the prize-winning book *All God's Dangers: The Life and Times of Nate Shaw*, a tale transcribed that now has been further transformed into a Broadway play.[3] H. Jack Geiger of the New York *Times* has called Cobb "a black Homer bursting with his black 'Odyssey.'" He was Ely's contemporary and the son of a sharecropper, fate of most former slaves in the heart of hard-scrabble Alabama. Rosengarten's friend had done what Booker T. Washington of Tuskegee advised for his race. Ned Cobb had "let down his bucket" where he was, from hard work prospered for a time, owned two mules, a Victrola, a decently furnished house, and a parcel of land. Yet, in defiance of racial rules and Washington's antiquated homilies, Cobb fought as hard as a lion-tamer for justice and personal vindication in the radical Sharecropper's Union movement during the 1930s and had to pay the penalty in material loss and imprisonment even if the effort gave him peace of mind. Ely had the same independent drive, sense of humor, native intelligence, and gift for words that Ned Cobb, though illiterate, brandished like cold-steel weapons. As these pages demonstrate, Green knew how to judge men and women, whatever the color of their skin, and make his moral points about their strengths and foibles in subtle but telling ways. Through the narrative art, both Green and Cobb rose above their circumstances not only to contribute a sense of dignity from which black Americans can draw enormous pride but also to advance the cultural life of their race, section, and nation.

Yet there are differences, too. Ely had a privileged—and ambiguous—upbringing. Its imprint upon his views separates him from the rebellious Alabama organizer. Indeed, as the son of an educated white man and a black house servant, Ely Green discovered his status in the rigid southern system much later than had Cobb, the unprotected child of a black sharecropper. Moreover, Cobb stayed largely in Alabama to struggle against the racial odds. For reasons this account reveals, Green had to flee his forest home to find his livelihood and full identity elsewhere. First he went to Wax-ahachie, Texas, where Oscar E. Dunlap, his employer and a wealthy judge, aided his effort to improve his education. Later Ely Green worked in California, where during the Second World War he helped to integrate the airplane man-ufacturing industry. The full autobiography describes these events in over six hundred printed pages.[4] Unlike Ned Cobb, who narrated his story, Ely Green painstakingly wrote the entire account himself, only later receiving the editorial assistance Arthur Chitty describes in his Afterword.

For a perhaps more appropriate analogy to this extraordinary memoir, one must turn to a second, equally powerful story, *The Narrative of the Life of Frederick Douglass, An American Slave*, in which the author told of his trials and intellectual growth in pre–Civil War Maryland. Tragically but also triumphantly, Green took a road toward freedom not unlike the one that Frederick Douglass had traversed in his courageous flight from his native habitat three quarters of a century earlier. Like Douglass, Ely Green owed something of his later, albeit modest, success in the white man's world to his lightness of color and to the paternalistic tradition in which he was raised. Both circumstances were psychically troubling yet deeply creative. Like Green, Douglass never learned for certain who his father, a white man, was. He barely knew his mother, who, like Green's, died early in his life. Yet, a succession of strong-minded and caring white and black folk, chiefly women, nurtured the young Douglass and admired his natural charm and alertness, traits that Ely Green also soon displayed. Douglass's grandmother performed an important role in his development of racial pride. But whites had helped him, too. Sophia Auld, a Baltimore slaveowner's wife, showed unusual compassion and kindly demeanor. She fired his ambition to read and write, though Douglass claimed in his memoir of 1845 that later her "angelic face gave place to that of a demon."[5] Nonetheless, her recognition of his special character and yearning for knowledge unwittingly encouraged his eventual self-discovery, a consciousness of worth which had made flight from slave brutality his inevitable course of action.

In Ely Green's narrative one finds the same kind of white sympathy, though racially and culturally constricted. With special recognition, for instance, he mentions not only the affection of his dying mother Lena Green and his older foster-sister, Ann (also a mulatto), but also "Mother Gerry" [Mrs. Guerry]. She was, he says, "just about the sweetest lady I ever knew" (p. 9). Unlike Douglass, however, the young Ely Green came to depend more on the favor of men like Churchill Eastin, William Alexander Guerry, and his own fiercely independent black grandfather Ned Green, a former slave, than he did on women of either race. At first, Ely Green had not understood his irascible elder. "These white men were so neatly dressed," he remarks, "and my grandfather was so dirty and greasy and smelled like slop" (p. 42). Ned was a self-employed hog-raiser, privy cleaner, and garbage collector. But gradually the child learned to love and appreciate him. "Boy, I want you to be a man like me," Grandpa Ned tells him. "You talk like these white people here in Sewanee. . . . Everybody that comes to Sewanee get all high-collared" (p. 98). The old man made a point that Ely Green did not forget.

Yet in this comparison with another black autobiographer, one again finds ironic differences. Although white, black, and possibly Native American blood flowed in his veins, Douglass did not mention the kind of suspicion in the slave quarters that Ely Green was to recount in the free black community of "Happy Hollow." That was the name insensitively bestowed by Sewanee's white employers on the tiny ghetto of shacks and muddy footpaths behind their comfortable houses. The children there called him "Clabber."[6] They refused to play with him. As a slave, Douglass shared the same woeful burdens that all others of that status endured, whatever the shade of their skin. Later, as a fugitive and freedman, he mingled on a level of relative equality with his northern reform-minded white and black friends who belonged to the "respectability," not the servant classes. Never was Ely Green to enjoy that advantage in later life. He was "too white, too black," just as Frederick Douglass was, but he was poorer and much more educationally disadvantaged throughout his life than Douglass had been over the course of years.

More important, Green's intention in writing his autobiography was what gerontologists call the process of "life review," the final act of identity that precedes death. In a scene from the longer work of which this is an excerpt, Green describes how in 1964 in Sewanee he visited eighty-four-year-old Dora Colmore, an employer for whom he had worked nearly a half century earlier. Although she was now half blind and crippled, Green's gesture "caused her to perk up, almost standing erect and representing the lady of dignity and character of true nobility."[7] In these chapters Ely Green has no political agenda, only the affirmation of life itself. The old man sought to bequeath something of himself for future generations in the hope that they would care.

Little known though he is, Green turns out to be more accurate and at least as sensitive a reporter of childhood events and feelings as the famous Douglass. Under William Lloyd Garrison's tutelage, the black abolitionist in his eloquent memoir composed the description of his slave boyhood when he was younger than thirty. Moreover, he did so to promote the cause in which he had so heartily enlisted. His recollections, still raw, were bound to be colored by that purpose.

In addition, the two autobiographers differed in their experiences with former white patrons. On the one hand, only later in life did Frederick Douglass fully acknowledge the role that some whites, including Sophia Auld, had played when he was young. In his senior years after the Civil War, the great orator, reformer, and Republican leader was surprised and naively hurt that his gestures of reconciliation toward white descendants of those who had befriended him met with sullen rebuff. They would not forget his former, publicized "ingratitude," necessary though it had been to arouse northern indignation in the bitter struggle for the emancipation of his race.[8]

On the other hand, Ely Green grew up in an atmosphere of Anglican noblesse oblige more rarified, more sentient than that which Douglass had known. Defeat in war, a desire to replicate an idealized version of "the old days," and uneasy consciences induced Sewanee Episcopalians to set a regional example of racial benevolence. The mulatto could never forget the kindness of his childhood patrons—the clergy and authorities like Major Archibald Butt, President Theodore Roosevelt's military aide. As Green recounts, Major Butt went down with the *Titanic* in 1912. He was a gentleman of the old school to the end. A rescued southern passenger reported that the kindly major had helped her into one of the last lifeboats, solemnly tipped his hat, and asked to be remembered to the folks at home. "I didn't know at this time," Ely was to write, "that the greatness of Sewanee would be my guide on the life journey, walking the path of tradition" (p. 226). "Aristocrats" he called his white elders with unselfconscious pride. Seldom do we unearth this kind of portrait from the recipients of upper-class largess. It may not be one that the average black received from the ruling race. Yet Ely Green's sincerity is all the more unquestionable because he does not fail to recognize the other side of the equation.

Certainly the pain that his equivocal upbringing as white, then black, comes through with an irony that readers, born to different standards of racial awareness, must supply for themselves. One suspects, however, that the memoirist intended it to be that way. In telling his impassioned story, Douglass pointed out that blacks often hid their feelings as a matter of self-protection. "They suppress the truth rather than take the consequences of telling it, and in so doing prove themselves a part of the human family."[9] Ely Green does not deliberately prevaricate in showing little overt bitterness when his white friends let him down. Instead, being the southern gentleman he was (I mean no irony here at all), he is reticent at a point when an angrier, more inner-directed writer, like Mississippi-born Richard Wright, would have fully voiced his feelings of outrage and frustration. Yet who can miss the poignancy of the little boy watching from a safe distance the cadets from the military academy as they marched in their Confederate-gray uniforms to Sunday service? In a comparable incident, during a winter Commencement Week, Green writes that he, sister Ann, and others, shivering in the cold, were watching the white people's entertainments through the windows. Then Telfair Hodgson invited the little group to sit in an inconspicuous spot inside. Ann was delighted. As the dancers moved about, she remarked on the stylishness of the girls on whom she waited every day of the festivities. "This was the first time I realized," Ely Green says, "something about me that was not fair—white people just let a Negro go so far and no farther, though we were a part of them and they were a part of us. Why were we at a handicap? No answer. I had worn out the patience of everybody asking questions" (p. 74). His understatement is exceptional. He is trying to be true to his feelings at this moment in his young life.

We must remember that Ely Green had composed his memoirs over many years, long before the upsurge of black consciousness was to reach its climax throughout the land in the 1960s. Yet, to mistake Ely Green for an "Uncle Tom" would be to rob him of his humanity, his highly developed sense of humane discrimination, his whole-souled uniqueness as both a black man and a white. To be sure, he was conservative. On his return to Sewanee, forty-five years later, at the Supply Store he carefully put on the old mask when queried by suspicious whites. He dismissed the Freedom Rider movement and added that he "didn't care for racial discussion, not in the South." At the same time, he firmly stated his business: "I was born in this town. I represent the melting pot of the U.S.A. My father was one of you aristocrats of this town. My mother was a colored woman. This has caused me to have to walk the third path of segregation."[10] He knew just how far he could test the chilly racial waters.

Certainly Ely Green held the same biases against poor-white mountain people in the area as the upper-class residents did. He labels them "sagers." The college people call them "covites." They could prove to be as mean as the young Douglass's succession of overseers had been. Like the antebellum Maryland slave, Green had reason to fear and distrust some, but by no means all, of his white neighbors. Fiercely proud of their skin and way of life, most of the small farmers of the mountain valleys had no use for the self-possessed Ely Green or any other blacks connected with the educated inhabitants of the cloistered enclave. Yet, even in the remotest coves, Green found heroes like Alf Cannon and John Atkins. They were brave men unwilling to bow to conventional racial custom.

Oddly enough, both Douglass and Ely Green in their later years returned to the scenes of their childhood. The pains of past wrongs had not been wholly erased, but they were somewhat dulled by the passage of years. Douglass visited Tuckahoe and the Eastern Shore of his youth. Fondly he recalled the good times as well as the nearly unbearable. So, too, Ely Green returned to "the Mountain" in old age. The circumstance made possible the publication of his memoir. The two autobiographers mourned not only missing friends of both races but their own lost youth, as, in Ely's case, the visit to Dora Colmore demonstrated.

On the edge of death, Frederick Douglass declared, "I remember that God reigns in eternity, and that, whatever delays, disappointments and discouragements may come, truth, justice, liberty, and humanity will prevail." Ely Green

xvi

not only believed that sentiment but also exemplified it in his life and in the telling of his moving story. Ironically, this tale of a mulatto's evolution toward adulthood, so long unfamiliar to the American public, illuminates the special predicaments of this class of racial victims about whom we know too little. Along with the works of those notables who wrote for the *Sewanee Review*, Ely Green's memoir belongs in the southern literary canon and merits a wide and enduring readership.

BERTRAM WYATT-BROWN

October 26, 1989

NOTES

1. C. Van Woodward, "The Irony of Southern History," in *The Burden of Southern History* (Baton Rouge: Louisiana State University Press, 1960), 167–91.

2. William Alexander Percy, *Lanterns on the Levee: Recollections of a Planter's Son* (1941; Baton Rouge: Louisiana State University Press, 1974), 93–94.

3. Geiger quoted in Patrick Pacheo, "A Black Homer Bursting with a Black 'Odyssey,'" New York *Times*, Theater Section, October 22, 1989, p. 5; Theodore Rosengarten, *All God's Dangers: The Life of Nate Shaw* (New York: Knopf, 1975).

4. Ely Green, *Ely: Too Black, Too White* (Amherst: University of Massachusetts Press, 1970).

5. Frederick Douglass, *The Narrative of the Life of Frederick*

Douglass, An American Slave, ed. Benjamin Quarles (1845; Cambridge, Mass.: Harvard University Press, 1960), 58.

6. Not because his wits were scrambled but because those of his white half-brother were.

7. Green, *Ely: Too Black, Too White*, 631.

8. See Dickson J. Preston, *Young Frederick Douglass: The Maryland Years* (Baltimore: Johns Hopkins University Press, 1980).

9. Douglass, *Narrative*, 43.

10. Green, *Ely: Too Black, Too White*, 629.

Introduction
by
Lillian Smith

Ely's town is a dream town. Dreamed up not by Ely but by the white South, and then created into actuality. A living thing: patterned by love, shaped by guilt and lust, colored by tenderness and awe, slashed by pride and greed, its boundaries strictly limited by an unspoken terror; the whole microcosm, indestructible in appearance, settling slowly, inevitably, into the trembling earth out of which it came.

White children of my generation felt the trembling if they lived on "the right side of town." For a colored child to feel the gusty sighs and sudden roars, hushed but awesome, that came out of the depths of this man-made Thing, this artifact of man's hungers and intelligence and longing to become something superior (even though this something might transgress the laws of nature and God), he, too, had to live on the "right side of town."

Ely Green came from the right side of town—in this case, the "right side" being the "corporation," called Sewanee, Tennessee, bounded by physical and psychological and economic and historical limits.

Across the South—from the deepest, darkest South to the hills of Appalachia—there have been these towns, created out of dream that more often than not turned into nightmare; a dream made in part of sickness and sin and in part of a terrible longing to become something better, bigger, finer, than human beings had ever been. The pathos of the South, and its tragedy, come out of the fact that the white man's image of what was "better" and "bigger" and "finer" was a gross, malignant distortion, an image in which the body acquired a hierarchic value above the soul.

In *Strange Fruit,* I wrote of such a town and its people. It was an imaginary story based on the experiences of a childhood lived on the edge of Georgia and Florida; in *Killers of the Dream,* I wrote autobiographically, critically, of the terrors and anguish, the destructiveness and beauty, the madness and sweetness and ugliness of this "trembling earth" on which all southern children of my generation grew up.

On the surface it was an uglier portrait of the southern way of life than is Ely's: Ely's is gentler, almost "charming" at times, and yet much more terrible. Ely's childhood was spread with a meringue of love—white people's love, white people's generosity, white people's superficial concern: a fluffy, sweet meringue which covered a pie made of ashes and dung and broken metallic bits of "history." The slave's history.

And Ely—bastard son of the son of a prominent white Sewanee family and a sensitive, lovely Negro girl—responded with all his hungry little heart to the gentle gestures of the upper-class whites, betrayed by his wistful curiosity concerning the "real world." The real world was for him the white world of this lovely Tennessee town: the only world, he thought—at age five and six and seven; the most exciting world, he thought—at age nine and ten and eleven, when the students of Sewanee's famed military academy made a mascot of him; a world to fight and despise, he thought—at age thirteen and fourteen, when he broke his heart against invisible barriers; an insane, mad world that drove him to want to kill, kill almost everybody, white and black, rich and poor—at age sixteen and seventeen, when finally he had to leave town to keep from being lynched.

Ely's story: told now in his old age: told with superb style, the style of one whose memory is as fresh and pure as it was in his childhood—unspoiled by the alphabet and the printing press. Misspelled words . . . oral disregard of syntax . . . these "errors" (a literate society calls them so) only enhance the story.

He is a fabulous storyteller. He has the power of hypnosis which every gifted storyteller has; he makes you believe; and I, knowing both the old and contemporary South, believe him willingly. Partly because he hypnotizes me, yes; but also because my mind knows, my life knows, that he speaks the truth.

Ely . . . telling us of a life gone forever; we know as we read that it is gone (Sewanee knows it, too, and will read, I hope without anger, of this long-gone time), and yet we also know its bittersweetness, its awesome chain of love, of disesteem, of hate and pride, is wrapped around every American mind. Not just the southern mind.

We could talk about Ely's story as a human document —and it is that, in a sense: a most extraordinary document, tender in its pathos, keen in its insight, exciting in its sudden anger and quick forgiveness of both races. This storyteller is not speaking about "civil rights." He is talking about man's future, and man's past, although he does not use such words. He is talking about girl, boy, man, woman, longing to relate to each other and this strange, shrinking world they live in; he is talking about the longing to feel that together we billions of human beings may find a way to deal with the enlarging cosmos we are becoming aware of. But Ely is not an intellectual; he could not possibly form such phrases; he could not talk of "the media of communication," or the electronic age, or man's need "to be in dialogue" with other men and his world; he does not talk about segregation as a human defense that is as dangerous as nuclear missiles; he does not analyze the times when a limited segregation can be used temporarily, briefly, as a human defense and when it is not only immoral but actually dangerous to use it—so dangerous it could blow up our earth, and may.

He does not think like this. He thinks stories. He could tell his story on the streets of Asia or India or Africa, as I have so often heard storytellers tell theirs, and soon there would gather round him the hod carriers and rickshaw coolies, the Untouchables and the cleaners, the beggars and poked-out-bellied street kids who would listen to his tale, strange to them in its details and yet as familiar to their hearts as their own body smells. For he would be telling them the oldest story on earth: "We are the forgotten ones; somehow we got here, no one knows quite how or why, and ever since we've been holding on; this is the way it happened in faraway America, in that fabulous and beautiful and ugly and awful part of it called the South. Somehow, I held on—but always my grip was slipping. This is what happened to me, and finally one day my fingers slipped."

In one sense this is such an old story of cruelty and blindness that it has become a stereotype; cleaned of its vivid, concrete details it could possibly change from a terrible experience to a cliché that you might turn away from.

But when Ely tells it, it is something told for the first time. This gifted man seems to have forgotten not one smell, not one tactile experience, not one blubby sound, or fleeting sight. His senses (wide-awake, as some say all of ours were before the printing press changed our world into a repetitive world of thin-leveled sightedness) reach out for every incident: we smell his grandfather's pigpen as we slip on its slime and our muscles jerk unforgettably; we hear those hogs grunt and see them slobber over the rotten slops from the summer boarding houses as we almost taste the putrid mess—and then, suddenly, something deeper-down than the senses is stirred by the ancient threat of the wild boar . . . but now, Ely has pulled us away to the hills, and we are smelling wild blossoms in the rain and trembling at the thunder; then suddenly, when Ely's leg is scratched by dirty barbed wire or a jagged splinter the wound goes beyond our own epidermis and dermis into our flesh and festers there as it does in his leg: but now, somehow the wound has healed and our hand, with his, is rubbing soft slick moss on a rotted log beyond the rush of icy mountain water and, as we lie there listening, smelling an earth millions of years old, we see, just beyond a thicket of green-black rhododendron, eyes staring. Are they man's eyes or animal's?

xxiii

Ely never knew for sure the name of his white father, although he knew the family and the family knew and accepted him on many levels. Let me qualify this: Ely knew and he didn't know. This white family was kind to him and concerned about him—as were their next-door neighbors, who seemed uncurious and completely accepting of the little fellow everyone called "adorable" and "dear." But his mother refused to name the father to Ely, although later Ely heard from his relatives that she kept in touch with him. Ely heard, too, that his father gave her a few pieces of fine jewelry, among them a ring of great value which she insisted must be left on her finger when she was buried. And it was left there, although Ely's Negro family was bitterly poor and could have used the money from that ring. But all of this is vaguely remembered by the small child and was never checked on by the grown-up man who had fled for his life at age eighteen. Everybody seemed to know something of vast importance to Ely, but Ely was never let in on the secret.

On this fine—in his eyes elegant—street, Ely did not have to go through back doors. Not for a long time. White faces smiled at him as he came up the front steps; white hands affectionately tousled his curly head; white voices were gentle and kind; white minds remembered a small boy's big appetite: "Ely, hello; come by for your dinner, we're having fried chicken and stewed corn and candied sweet potatoes and peach ice cream; if you come in time you can finish freezing the ice cream and can lick the dasher." And Ely, like thousands of other southern children, white and dark, couldn't resist licking the "dasher" of the old-fashioned ice-cream churn. And then he'd stay

xxiv

for his dinner. The cook would heap lots of it on a big plate, and he'd sit there on the comfortable broad back porch or at the big kitchen table where "help" and family were going back and forth, and eat his dinner. "Oh, but he didn't eat in the dining room with the white family!" your mind may say. No, he didn't. And for years, he wouldn't have wanted to; it never occurred to him; it was a *modus vivendi* that satisfied everybody. Neither whites nor blacks raised questions.

Sometimes, one of the white ladies, while out driving her beautiful pair of horses, would see Ely idling on the street, sauntering along with a specific destination in mind perhaps, or perhaps only a vague one. She would stop her carriage, call to him, "Hop in, Ely." Ely would hop in, she would ask him where he wanted to be put out, he would tell her, and often she would drive half a mile out of her way to leave him where he wanted to be. Likely as not, as he jumped out and thanked her, she'd reach down and pat his curly head, as she murmured, "You have lovely manners, Ely; you are going to grow up to be a fine boy, I can see it." And as she drove away, Ely would admiringly watch her—for these beautiful women were expert with their horses—and his heart would swell with pride in her and himself (he felt a close bond between them) and he would resolve that he'd never forget his nice manners and he *would* grow up to be a fine boy. For at this time, Ely saw only this dream South—mythic, yes; a fantasy, yes; but real, too, slivery real, one might say, for there was real affection felt by these people for Ely; and he felt real affection for them; they were concerned about him, and he was as concerned as a small boy can be about them. And he didn't know then that a day would come when he would want to kill all the white people in the world and maybe all the colored people, too, and maybe himself, as this charming, elegiacally lovely Sewanee turned into a shriveling, rotten Earth whose inhabitants, all of them (or nearly all) seemed to despise its children, especially those who didn't know the names of their white fathers.

But hate had a difficult time growing in Ely's heart. The first five years of his life were too crowded with love —especially the love the "nice white folks" seemed to feel for this baby, this small toddler who apparently belonged to everybody. That he actually belonged to nobody was just too absurd to think about for more than a few seconds at a time. And Ely would brush off the feeling (it was feeling, not idea).

If he felt ill at ease with anybody in his baby years, it was black folks. Things were not good in his black family. His mother was dead. Kinfolks had taken him in. They were poor, hard-working people who couldn't answer his questions. They were often sick. They had outbreaks of rage, at times. But Ely was fast growing used to gentle words, quiet, soft voices, good food, bright toys, and chummy little white faces. He played in the front yards with these little whites; he sat in the company of elegant ladies who at times affectionately admired him. He was Sewanee's Pet. But at night he left the security of the corporation and went out to the colored section—yet there was something in this black family that he loved and respected, even though he often found their life unendurable; he clung to them with a touching fidelity.

"We love our colored folks," upper-class whites in the South always said and felt virtue growing in hearts and minds like a delicate flower, as they spoke these strange words. Ely was "ours." Ely belonged. If Mrs. So-and-So saw him in a pair of worn-out pants she scolded him softly, "You must always look nice, Ely dear; you mustn't go dirty." Then she'd see that Ely was given some spotless and well-cared-for but secondhand pants and shirts to wear. And Ely would proudly dress up in his secondhand clothes, which looked almost as though they'd just come from the store in a bright package, and he would be proud of how nice he looked, and proud of his nice manners, and proud of all his white friends, especially the cadets at the school, which Ely was sure someday he, too, would attend for everybody there was so nice to him.

But one day, this life streaked with fantasy and reality turned over just a little; just enough to show its dark, festered belly. Ely had to leave the corporation where he had spent his days, and go to the edge of town where the poor whites and poor blacks lived not too far from each other, and go every morning to "school." He didn't want to go. But he went—and received his first massive cruelty from these impoverished black children. They jeered him, they called him "Clabber" and "bastard"; he was to them no real Negro and no real white; they wouldn't play with him; he was given the full treatment human beings accord to the rejected. The rejection, brutal and total, coming not from whites but from Negroes, was more than he could take. He despised them. He was outraged. He was insulted. Later Father Eastern—Sewanee is still known today as an Episcopal Church center—who was Ely's priest (yes, in

Sewanee, Ely was a good Episcopalian with a white priest who cared for him) was to talk to him about school. "You must go to school, Ely. You have a good mind, you must learn to read and write; you must get an education." But something always happened to postpone Ely's return to school.

Thus, slowly, oh so creepingly, Ely began to feel that Something Was Very Wrong with his world—and it wasn't entirely due to people with black faces. For he was by now also discovering the poor whites, stiff with envy of the upper-class whites and fearful of "niggers," poor whites who lived outside the "real" Sewanee, just as did the colored folks beyond the corporation.

Only the "nice whites" lived within that fabulous enclave in the last decades of the nineteenth century and the first decades of the twentieth. The town's barrier was not invisible as it was in my small Deep South town but actually *there.* Beyond the limits of the corporation the rejected lived, white and black. You, if you were "nice," spent your life within this Sewanee segregated from "the others." "Your" nice colored people came in early every morning—some lived in and were part of the enclave; they were encouraged to dress up, "not only on Sunday," Ely tells us, "but every day." They were praised when they did. The Negro men houseservants wore white shirts and ties and coats. These white people were very proud of their colored servants, Ely tells us. "I have heard them, even the schoolboys, criticize the poor sagers for the way they look. They wouldn't even *look* at them." (The "sagers" were the poor whites.)

There was, apparently, in Ely's town as much segregation practiced against the poor whites as against the ordinary Negroes. The "chosen Negroes" were treated in a very special way that is difficult, even for one familiar with southern nuances of behavior, to categorize. Man's mind has set up very special categories that fit no words: these chosen Negroes were not treated as highly valued and beloved dogs—as we sometimes say when outraged by the twists and turns of racism. They were always human beings to the whites, who cherished and disesteemed them simultaneously, but beings limited subtly in their humanity. Perhaps women should understand—as throughout thousands of years of patriarchy they, too, however beloved and petted and cherished, have been stripped of their human rights and their men's esteem. And yet, women know they are not in men's minds pushed into a category with animals; however bitter they may become, however brutally treated or obscenely spoken of, they know this.

And Ely, now an old man, knows this, too. And as he remembers his strange, almost fantastic, life, he never loses the knowledge for more than a brief span of time that the ideas and illusions of the white man about the black race are complex and intricately involved with his ideas about his own body image, his own sense of self or non-self. He understands a great deal about the murky depths of the human heart. He knows well that bestiality, cruelty, hate, contempt, greed, and indifference to suffering are not qualities limited to the white race but are feelings, attitudes, that all men experience and must deal with. He knows there is an evolutionary pull toward complexity in the human race—knows it intuitively—but he knows also that there is a drift, an earthwide drift, that pulls mankind backward, also. Never can Man reverse the evolutionary pull, but he can block it and detour it. And hate increases the regressive power of this backward drift.

Ely's knowledge—gained from a lifetime of close observation of his fellow men—oozing out of his pores, one might say, has served him well. Hate would have torn his story to pieces; lies would have flooded the fissures left by such hate—and we should have had from him only another of the paranoid "autobiographies" which have been pouring from the presses in recent years. These books tell us, with monotonous perseveration, that racism kills bodies, yes, and kills the spirit of men; and we know this is true—but not in the sense that Ely's story is true. Ely's truth is that of the artist and the poet (unlettered, yes); a truth discovered by his whole organism. Ely's capacity for love and forgiveness (amazing gift!), his talent for understanding psychological complexities, safeguard him from the lying generalizations that pour out so easily from a raging mind. Love can distort truth, too (it more often drowns it, I think)—as can fear; and I am sure both have twisted Ely Green's acts and feelings throughout his life, as did his rages during adolescence, which now he sees so clearly. And yet, as he tells us his story, he seems to have escaped almost entirely the traps of self-pity and the habit of crude generalizations. He is not writing about "the Negro" and "Mr. Charlie" or "Whitey" or "the white race," or the "white imperialists": he is telling us a strange, frightening, tender, often beautiful, and more often brutal story of one boy, from birth to age eighteen, who lived in one town—a town like every other southern town in that it shared a common history, an economic deprivation, an unending moral struggle, and memories of war and reconstruction, but unlike most towns in that it was inhabited by people with power who were unusually capable of compassion, apparently unpoisoned by uncontrolled defensiveness, and possessed of the gentle manners and good will that southerners have always boasted of and so rarely have actually had.

Perhaps as much as anything else Ely's story will remind us that there is a structural, bony sameness throughout the region that can be called accurately "the South"; but it is fleshed out in ten thousand different ways—ways often strikingly inconsistent with the "beliefs" that seem inherent in the structure.

Young Ely could not possibly have "made up" the tender-minded, warm, generous, often highly intelligent people in his book; they existed, yes; but side by side with their softness, warmth, generosity, and concern for "their Negroes" was a blindness, a complacent ignorance of human growth, an almost complete refusal to look toward a future where all human beings would have their rights and be relatively free at least to become complex, interesting people. Such words would never have entered their heads. This blindness stuns the sensitive modern reader—and yet why should it? It is Ely Green's talent that makes readers see, as though it were an exotic growth, what is flourishing lushly now at our feet.

Just as their town of Sewanee was split into fragments, so their minds were split. Conscience from heart and soul, and past from future. A highly schizophrenic existence: a play that never ended produced on a stage that seemed never to wear out, acted by the audience itself: unreal, theatrical, often full of dark humor, often ingratiating; but after a time, the actors mistook the script for "real" life. In childhood little Ely strutted his part in it, proud to come on stage, proud to play the role "they" chose for him to play. Until, slowly—but far more rapidly than it occurred to the powerful, white actors—he saw it as a terrible drama, one he was doomed to act the same role in forever and ever. Unless he walked out, unless maybe he tore the whole theater down in his hurt and rage.

The slaves in the United States had less legal protection from the greed and brutalities of their owners than those of any other civilized country in the world. For thousands of years slavery had been (and still is) a common thing throughout the world among primitives and the highly civilized—ever since man discovered how to use and exploit the amazing energies of his fellow men, which he found were superior to animal energy and cheaper to sustain. Slavery continued until the machine gave men something more powerful to exploit and to be exploited by. But nowhere in all the world has there been, side by side with the ruthless disregard and the cruelty and greed, so much tender concern for individual slaves, as much warm affection for "our Negroes," as here in the South. Love and disesteem, concern and cruelty, patience and hideous punishment, all interwoven and interlocked until the southern mind was imprisoned in a swamp of evil and good, of destruction and creativity and love and hate and security and *angst*.

Call it swamp; call it a crisscross of chasms; call it labyrinth—call it any metaphor you choose that cuts or blocks a man's relationship with his soul and self and future and you have what happened to the whites. And in a different way the slashing of the Negroes' life was worse: physically much worse, economically worse. I doubt that Negroes were as injured spiritually by this way of life as were the whites. It is difficult to measure spiritual degradation, almost impossible to compute the spread through a human organism of a contagious disease like "white supremacy." But as one reads this book, focusing on one little boy, then as years passed, on one wiry young adolescent, now and then one looks up from the book and ponders this terrible problem of what a fragmented, segregated life can do to the human spirit. What it can do to a whole civilization. What detours it can compel evolving mankind to make on his journey toward his future.

Ely Green leaves the questions to us, for the most part. Here and there, in a few pithy words, he sums up in unforgettable language years of degradation, centuries of human arrogance. He knows the depths. He, thank God, was able at times to glimpse the future; almost like a visionary he would see it. Some of his wisdom came from his earthy and at times half-drunken grandfather; some of it came from the sensitive, deeply feeling Father Eastern, who knew only too well what was ahead of this young boy. This white priest was a man of profound spiritual insight, possessing humor and patience and warmth; he, like a few other white southerners, knew the evil we lived, suffered from it, and yet felt unable to fight the dragon called "southern tradition"—and I am not sure that at his time of history he could have done in Tennessee much more than he did. But I am glad Ely Green tells us about him.

But Ely had to fight *his* personal and cultural dragons all by himself; he chose interesting weapons, and these he tells about in his story. His brief flight to the hills at age sixteen, his learning to be one of the best shots with a rifle that the region knew, his friendship with young hillmen, some of whom were moonshiners, some poachers who trapped fur-bearing animals in order to sell the skins—all this Ely tells about; none was better at this poaching game than Ely himself; and here, white and Negro found common needs and common outlets for both poverty and their inner aggressions. He loved the hills and he writes beautifully of them—saying that only in the hills did he feel a free man.

Much of Ely's life was totally unlike the old stereotypes that people in the past have written of, and that nearly all Americans think in terms of, when thinking or talking about "the South" or "the Negro" or "the poor white." Perhaps one reason the book is so fascinating is that we feel nuances we have been unaware of; we guess at actions we had not dared think southerners were capable of; we learn that the differences between each of us are terribly important to cherish even though we value more and more our common humanity. And we learn this in a subliminal fashion as we listen to Ely's soft voice telling a tale that sends shivers down the spine.

LILLIAN SMITH

"On the Mountain"
Clayton, Georgia
May, 1966

xxxiv

ELY

CHAPTER

1

I was born in 1893 in a small town in Tennessee—Sewanee, location of the University of the South.

My father was a white man, my mother a so-called Negress. I was looked on as a half-white bastard, and called that by almost everyone that knew me.

In Sewanee many of the better class of white people often taken Negro boys and girls into their homes to train them to be effecient help. This is how my mother became a victim of misfortune by producing me when she was seventeen. When she discovered she was pregnent her mistress sent her away for me to be born.

After I was born my mother was taken in by the family of Dr. Richerson who lived on the next estate to my father's people. I have never known why that kind couple should have been so thoutful to my mother. They treated her as if she was one of the family. When I was two years old my mother married and brought me to live on the estate with her and her husband.

I was about three years old before I can remember things that went on about me. My stepfather was a fine man. He was good to me, although I became to know that he was not my father at four years old—Christmas, 1897.

Most days my mother taken me up to Mother Richerson's when she went to work. I would play all over the house. Mother Richerson was very fond of me. She done lots of handwork. When I would do things wrong she would say: "I dropped a stitch. Find it." I would crawl over the floor hunting for the stitch while both mothers would laugh.

That Christmas there was to be company for dinner, so my mother thought I would be in the way of the guests. She explained to me that Santa Claus had brought me some fireworks and toys. I was most happy.

She ask me to stay in the servants' quarters until after dinner and not to touch the fireworks. She dressed me in a little plaid dress and told me to stay in the house. It was bitter cold outside, and there was snow on the ground. The drum stove was red hot when she left for work. She came back every hour to see how I was.

The stove was red from heat. Holding a roman candle in my hand, playing with it, I let it touch the stove until it lighted and started to sparkle. I tried to put it out. It set my dress afire. I ran to the door and threw the candle out. I was on fire. Not knowing what to do I leapt in the bed and covered it which put the fire out.

Later, I got up and changed my dress and hid the burned dress in the box where I kept my clothes. Mother came with my dinner. Most cooks down South feed their children from the white folks' kitchens. This is called "toten."

She had some toys and a lot of nickels that Mother Richerson and her guests had sent me. While she was placing my dinner on my little table, she smelled the burnt

4

cloth. She ask me what had happen. She wanted to know if I had used any of my fireworks. I told her "No."

Soon she found I had lied. This was the first time I remember of being whipped by her. When she stopped whipping me I ran out in the snow screaming so loud that she had to try to run me down to get me back in the house. Before she could reach me I had crawled through the bars of the big gate to the adjoyning estate that belonged to my father's people.

I stood screaming. My mother stood coaxing me to come back to her. She didn't wish to come through the gate. Some one spoke from behind me: "What are you whipping him for?" Mother replied: "He lied to me and I spanked him and he ran away from me."

A white lady taken me by my hand, led me to the gate, and told my mother to take me in the house and come back to the gate because she had something for me at her house. So mother taken me in and told me to stay until she came back.

She came back with lots of oranges and candy and toys. She told me: "These were sent to you." I ask her: "Who is the lady?" She looked at me for a moment, and said: "You might as well know now. That was your grandmother of your white family. She said for you to be a good boy and don't tell stories to anyone."

It made me very happy to think someone else loved me, too. No farther did I think of it. Later, my stepfather came and helped me shoot my fireworks. I was so fond of him. I didn't have any children to play with. I only had my mother and father. They were like two pals.

We didn't have any company except my father's

friends that worked on the construction. When it rained the men often came to the house to play checkers. My stepfather was a good player. No one had anything much to say to me. I was always busy trying to build something or make something.

When my mother was off the job she started me on my alphabet. I was four years old. I had to count everything that came in the house—from my father's pay envelope to the matches in boxes. Sometimes I would complain. She would tell me that she wanted me to be the best educated man in world.

When I would go up to Mother Richerson's house I had to do the same thing. When I was four and a half Mother Richerson bought me a slate and started me writing. She also told me I had to be baptized.

Father Gerry came the next day with Bishop Gailor and Father Claiborne. When they taken me in the parlor I became frighten and tried to run out. My mother caught me and held on to me.

The Fathers had on their carters and gowns which I had never seen. Mother Richerson and Bishop Gailor knelt by me, and he told me I was a child of God and must be baptized. The Bishop would be my Godfather, Mother Richerson would be my Godmother, and Father Gerry and Father Eastern would be my counselmen.

I was most happy to know that I had so many friends. I began to love everybody.

I wish to explain something about Sewanee—why the white people there were so democratic. Most people at that time who lived in Sewanee were of English descent. Many were of nobility respected in England. The residential area was fenced in. No poor white people lived inside the fence. Nobody lived there except the aristocrats and their servants —housemaids, butlers, coachmen. The servants were all colored, and most everyone was called colored. You rarely ever heard the words used—Negro or nigger. It seemed that everybody was happy just to be there.

When I was five years old my little brother was born. I became jealous immediately. It seemed everything changed in every way. People came to our house to see my little brother. Everyone colored was so fond of him. Until this happened few women ever came to see my mother. There were but few ever had anything to say to me. They would just look at me as if I could not have been.

My white family was named Doane. Some of the women would say to the others: "He sure is a Doane. He's just like them." By the time I was six years old I had become to understand that I just wasn't like the rest of my family. I know my mother had become to notice my feelings though she didn't say anything to me concerning them.

I was given more priviledges. I was allowed to go out in the park and play with the white children, when their nurses brought them in the park to play. Many times the mothers would come with their children. They were all so kind to me.

The town was so small that the streets didn't have any names. No houses had any numbers. Everybody knew everybody, black or white. The white people had everything under such control. It seemed that everyone knew me and was so kind to me. Often they would bring ice cream and cookies. I would be sirved with their children. This went on for about six months.

Then my mother told me that school was opening out of the corporation, and I should go. This was where most of the colored people and the poor class of white lived. On the first day she taken me to school so I would know the way. I met the teacher and was enrolled. For two weeks I went to school. I did not like school because the children didn't like me. I was the only real light-complected one in the school.

The rumer soon was out that I was a bastard and that my white uncle was a nitwit who was called a clabber. Soon all the children poked fun at me for this name which vexed me very much. My teacher was very kind until I started to fight the kids when they would tease me. I was graded and placed in the second reader.

Just as I was beginning to become adjusted my mother taken sick. She wanted me to stay with her. She had been ailing ever since my brother was born. She never went back to work. I was glad not to go to school.

My mother was aflicted with consumption. She know she would never be well. For four months before she got too weak she kept me with her almost every minute.

Sometimes she would take me and my brother up on the main street when the military students would march by. I thought that was the greatest something that could be—to be a cadet. Sunday morning the cadets would march to music by their band like the West Point cadets. I would go just two blocks from St. Augustus Chapel and try to keep up with them until they got to the Chapel. At the Chapel they would pass in review and salute their superiors. I would stand and salute, too.

Everybody always waited for the arrival of the cadets before going in the Chapel. When they marched in I would go to the back of the Chapel to watch the organ pumper pump the pipe organ. After a few Sundays I was spoken to by many white people. All white people down South seems to love colored children.

One morning there was a package left on our doorstep. I brought it in and gave it to my mother. She open it. There was a little coat and cap something like the cadets wore. So Sunday mornings I would wait for the cadets to pass. Everybody would laugh. When I pass by they would salute me. I do believe those were the happiest days of all my life.

Very soon my mother became so sick that I could not wait on her. My stepfather had to get a woman to care for her. I had my little brother to look after. My stepfather built another room on to the one we had been living in where we cooked, slept and bathed. Father Gerry came every morning with Dr. Hall. Father Gerry would pray and before he would leave he would tell me to stay close to my mother. Many white people would drive up in carrages bringing something for her. They were generous in every way.

One morning Father ask me to go home with him. He only lived a block from us. This was the first time I had gone to any white home. We went in. He had three children: Alexander, Annie and Sumner. His wife, whom he called Mother, taught kindergarten.

Almost everyday except Sunday I would go home with Father to play with the children at recess. Sometimes I stayed all night. Mother Gerry was just about the sweetest lady I ever knew. I did not attend her class although she explained anything I ask her and treated me like other children. This made me very happy.

I hadn't ever seen my mother go to church nor my

9

stepfather. One morning before Father Gerry came Mother ask me not to go over to the Gerry home. Elder Trouble was coming and I might be needed. He arrived with four women. They sang and prayed for many hours. All at once there was a scream. I knew it was my mother's voice. I rushed in the house. My mother was sitting up in bed, clapping hands, saying: "Glory hallalula, I been born again!" I rushed to her. She said: "My son, I am now happy." I didn't know what it all meant.

As I looked at all six people with tears streaming down their faces Mother held out her hands, saying: "Bring my two sons to me." I turned around to get my brother who was crawling in the door. I carried him to the bed. One of the women put him in the bed, and I climbed in. Mother, feeble as she was, pulled us both against her brest, fell back on her pillar, and said: "God bless them. I can now die happy." She ran her feeble fingers through my curls, saying over and over: "He leadeth me through green pastures and he lay me down by still waters. I will not fear to enter the valley of death. I will not be alone." Soon she was in a coma. I was told that Mother had confessed religion.

When the colored people had gone, Father Gerry came, and walked to her bedside. With his left hand he stroked her brow speaking softly words I can't remember. He knelt by the bed with me and the nurse, and prayed and talked with her.

Mother spoke, asking him what should be done with Ely. "I know I am going to die. Eddie has a father to look after him. Ely as he is, you know, hasn't anyone. I can die happy when I know that he will be cared for."

Father spoke, saying: "Lena, you know that Bishop

Gailor is Ely's Godfather, and I am his counselor with Father Eastern. He will be taken care of. Who do you think he could live with?" Mother told him to send for Matty Davis whom she had lived with when she was a girl. Father waited until I went for her and came back. It was agreed that Matty Davis would raise me. My mother was very happy. Father Gerry told Mother Matty that she would have help if she needed it.

That was the beginning of a new life for me. I left with Mother Matty. It was the last time I saw my mother alive. She died the next day.

My foster mother cooked for Dr. Barton. They let her keep me on the estate. I was allowed to go almost anywhere I wanted to go. Mother Matty had three grown children: one girl, two boys. She owned the house where they lived. None of them were married. I came to love her and her daughter as if they were my own.

Often I would go to the building where my stepfather worked to see him. He moved out of the corporation and married again. I loved him. He loved me, too, I knew. Everybody that knew him loved him, white or black. He was so strong I just loved to be close to him. He was said to be the strongest man in the county. He would display his strenth by lifting things to amuse the students. His job mostly was to wind the derick for the stone setters.

As I was turning nine, things began to change for me and happiness faded. All this time my friendships had broadened. Almost every notable in town knew me. Many of them would stop on the street and talk to me. I was taught by Mother to be courteous to everyone. I hadn't ever thought anything about race destinction. I knew little about colored children. The word Negro was rarely ever used, or I just didn't pay any attention to it. I had a dream that someday I would be like the students. I would be a cadet. All the white kids talked of this. We drilled and played together happily.

CHAPTER

2

One morning I went to Mother Gerry's to play. Mother said to us: "The leaves has blown over the yard. If you boys will rake them up I will give you fifteen cents each." The job was soon done. Out to the drugstore we went to buy an eggflip, a drink like a malted milk. Alexander, Sumner and I. We went to the dispencer and ordered three drinks. We had been here before many times and got drinks. Dr. Conger, the propiator, never said anything.

This day there was a new dispencer that I hadn't seen before. He made two drinks, handed one to Alexander and one to Sumner. I ask: "Where is my drink?" He said: "You don't get any." Alexander spoke up: "Why don't Ely get a drink? He has money to pay for it." The dispencer said: "I don't make drinks for no nigger. He is a nigger." Alexander said: "He is one of us." The dispencer said: "I wouldn't make a drink for a nigger if I never worked." The boys both tossed their glasses over the counter, and out of the store we went, back home. This was the first time I ever felt hurt, except when my mother died.

We didn't talk at all on the way home. When we entered the house Alexander and Sumner went strait to their room. I walked to the libiary where Mother Gerry and

Annie were sitting by the gratefire. Mother Gerry looked up and said: "Did you have a nice drink?" I said: "No, I didn't have a drink. The clerk wouldn't make me a drink. He called me a nigger and said he did not make drinks for niggers."

Mother stop looking at me and look toward the fire. I stood there for a moment. Then I ask her: "Mother, what is a nigger?" She did not answer. She walked to the hall and called the two boys to come to the libiary. She said: "I have some cookies and will make some hot choclate. You don't have to go to the drugstore." No one said anything.

She went to the kitchen. I followed her. While she was heating the milk I could see that she was a bit purturbed. Then I ask her: "Please tell me what is a nigger? Why should I be called a nigger. It must be very bad to be a nigger." She stood with her back to me fully a minute before she turned and faced me. She said: "Ely, I think this is a job for Father. You go to him. He can explain this better than I can. He is over at St. Augustus." For three years I had been coming to her for understanding. This was the first time she refused to explain something to me. I did not wait for choclate. I went over to St. Augustus.

Father Gerry was in his study, writing. He look up and said: "Ely, my boy, what brings you here?" I said: "Father, there is something I want to ask you if you have time." He said: "Have a seat there. I'll talk to you in a minute." I waited. He said: "Now what is it you want to know, Ely?" I stood up. "Father, I want to know, what is a nigger? I was called that by the clerk at the drugstore. He would not take my money. Mother Gerry said I should come to you for explanation."

He started to say something and stopted and sat for a moment. Then, he said: "Ely, I am very busy. I have this lecture to do so I will send you to Father Eastern. Tell him I sent you and he will explain to you what you need to know. If you don't find him at home come back tomorrow and I will talk to you." I thanked him and left.

This was the first time I had visited Father Eastern at home, though he often talked to me when he would meet me on the street. He was very fond of children. He was older than any of the Fathers. I did not feel as close to him as I did to Father Gerry. I wasn't sure that he would take time to talk to me like Father Gerry. I went into the yard. There were many pigeons on the lawn feeding on food he had thrown out to them.

He called to me, saying: "Ely, my boy, you have come to see me." He was standing in the doorway. He said: "Come in the house where it is warm." We went in his libiary. He ask how my foster mother was. I didn't care to talk as usually.

I said: "Father, I was sent here by Father Gerry for you to tell me what a nigger is and why should I have to be called a nigger?" He walked over to the window and stood looking out on the lawn. I spoke again, saying: "Father, have I done something wrong?" He turned to me, and said: "I want to think a bit. No, Ely, you haven't done any wrong." He had his robe on. He had never been married, and lived alone. He was a man in his sixties. Several minutes passed before he spoke again, laying his robe over the back of a chair. He said: "Ely, just you and I will take a walk down to the brook."

He put on his coat and hat, taken his cane, and we went

out to walk. He spoke about the birds enjoying their food. Then, we walked a hundred yards, and he hadn't spoke a word. Then, he started to talk of how beautiful the autumn was. The trees were beautiful. He continued to talk of nature. By this time it seemed as if I was closer to him than anyone else. No one of the white people had ever talked to me this long at one time. All fear had left me.

I ask him again: "Father, are you going to tell me what a nigger is?" He said: "What happened to you that you are so confused over the word?" I explained that I was called this name and was refused to be sold a drink at the drugstore. The clerk served the other children, and said he would not make a drink for a nigger—never. The other boys told him that I was one of them, but he would not listen to them. He said a nigger had no right to drink where white people drink.

Father said: "Let's sit here on this rock."

He said: "Ely, this has perturbed you very much, I know. I can see that. It may take sometime for you to understand the full meaning of this word nigger. But first I must correct that word. The word is Negro. Why it is trying for you is because you have been raised up here within about ten blocks in the corporation. You have been treated like all other children. You go to any home where there are children and you are accepted. Now don't let this burden you too much. You will see that it won't make any difference to people that love you." Then, he said: "You must come and talk to me more often. You know I am supposed to look after you. I was appointed by Bishop Gailor, who is your Godfather, as one of your counsellors. You can come to me anytime."

16

I said to him: "Father, I still don't know what a nigger really is." By this time we were back to the house. He looked up at the sky, and said: "You had better be going to your Mama Mat," as he called her. "It is getting late for you. Come back tomorrow after lunch and we can talk again. Forget about the clerk because he should not have talked to you that way."

On the way to Dr. Barton's I met many white ladies that I knew. Everyone spoke to me, saying "Hello, Ely," just as they had always done. I didn't tell my mother anything about what had happened. That day she was not much for talking. She believed in children being seen and not heard. On the way home she said: "Why are you so quiet tonight?" I had always been singing or jabbering away or asking questions which she seldom answered.

When we got home there was company. I went upstairs to bed. I could not go to sleep for a long time thinking about having to be a nigger. What could a nigger be and why should God make a nigger? I knew there were more to it than Father Eastern told me. I would learn more tomorrow when I go back to talk to Father.

The next morning it was raining and cold. Mama Mat and I went to work. We were soaked by the time we walked the half mile. I had to stay in the house all that day. Sitting there watching my mother make biscuits, which she was somewhat an artist at, beating the dough with a laundry iron. She let me beat some, too. Helping her gave my mind a lift. At two o'clock was her rest period. All the cooks were at liberty until five o'clock when they would go back to work to prepare dinner. They would often visit one another.

This day several maids came to visit my mother. There had been a lynching in Chattanooga. The victim was a Negro by the name of Ed Johnson. These maids were very much in distress over it. This was the first time I had been around when they were talking anything of rachel terms. This was the first time I had heard anyone talk about how badly the Negro could be treated. One of these maids I called Aunt Lula Gray. She was telling them about how loyal the Negro is to the white. A Negro had even knocked down the white man that shot and killed President McKinerly. They conversed their whole period of rest. I sat there listening to their conversation and whims.

That night Mama Mat and I stayed on the estate because it was raining. The next morning the sun came out bright. I could go out to play with the children if I so wished. I had decided I would not go back to Father Gerry's to play for awhile. There was something that wasn't just right in my feeling. The coachman was polishing the carriage when I heard the yells of the children playing at Father Gerry's home. It was recess. I found I was on my way there.

I had almost forgotten what had happened previous at the drugstore. When I arrived there were many children playing football. I had been one of the players on one of the teams, and much favored before this day. Just as I started to walk onto the lawn someone kicked the ball, and it landed just in front of me. I picked it up, intending to kick it. A boy name Randolph snatched the ball from me, and said: "This ball belongs to me. I did not buy this ball for a nigger to kick." It seemed that every boy there turned his back to me except Alexander, Father's oldest boy. He looked so unhappy. Soon they all forgot I was there.

I began to think how things had changed in just two days after this clerk had named me a nigger. I turned and went back to where my mother worked. I was hurt worse by this than ever before. All I could think was: "How could God make a nigger, and why?" Now I could cry a bit.

I went strait to the stable where Frank, the coachman, was cleaning out the stables. I tried to talk to him. He only looked at me like all other Negroes would when I would ask what was a nigger. It seemed there must be an answer somewhere. I could not give up trying. I thought of Father Eastern. He had told me to come to him anytime I wish to talk to him.

When I arrived at his home he was just returning from his walk after lunch. We met at the gate. He spoke to me so kindly, and invited me in the house. He often hummed a bit. I sat on the leather couch. He pulled off his coat, hung it in the closet, and put on his robe. Ten minutes passed and he was still humming very low. I sat there waiting for him to say something. I waited a few more minutes, then I spoke, saying: "Father, please tell me why there should be Negroes?"

He was looking at some papers on his desk. He drop the papers on the desk, turned to me, and said: "Are you still confused over that word?" I answered: "Yes, sir." He said: "Don't be." He spoke this like it was a command. I stood up, tried to talk, and then I bursted out crying, asking him: "Please tell me why our God would make anybody a nigger when no one liked them." I had put my face in my hands bending down on the couch crying. I felt his soft fat hands resting on my head. He was saying something.

The first thing I understood him to say was: "We are all God's children." He sat down on the couch still patting my head. He ask me to sit up. Then he said: "Ely, I didn't think this meant so much to you. You are so young to feel like this. What has happened?" I tried to talk. I began to tell him about what happened when I went to play with the children that morning. How Randolph refused to let me kick his football, and other boys did not want to play with me. How he called me a nigger. "Father, we have been playing together for two years. Since that clerk called me a nigger everyone else here thinks I am no good. What will I do?" I ask him why did people burn Negroes like they do. He ask who had burned anyone. I told him of what I had heard the maids talking about the lynching in Chattanooga.

He said: "Don't talk of this anymore. Don't burden yourself with things you hear like that. I have been much concerned about you since you came to see me. Ely, you are more advanced than I had given you credit to be. You caught me much unaware the other day. Now I will explain to you why there are Negroes. You will see that it is not at all bad to be called a Negro."

He started to talk. He told me the race which is called Negro was brought to the United States from Africa as slaves to serve the economy purposes of the white people. They were given the name Negro, which represents the word negroid, which has the latent meaning black. They were the descendants of a tribe in Africa named Negri on the Negro River. This happened over a hundred years ago.

20

At that time tyrant law was legitimate almost around the world. These men and women were sold at auction just like anything of material would be sold. Tyrant means ownership of man as property.

Then he said: "I was talking to your grandfather, Ned, who is the scavenger for the city. He was doing some work here for me yesterday. I had quite a talk with him. He was born in slavery. Sold on the block. Most of his family was sold like he was. He said some of his people had never been located yet. The government freed your people by a revolution called the Civil War, which freed the slaves. But the black people maintained the name Negro. In the Southern states mostly there is discrimination that supports segregation. This is very much a law. Anyone that has Negro blood in him is a Negro. It doesn't matter how white they are. They just don't have the priviledges that the white race has, especially in the South. These priviledges are limited even in law. Although it may seem very unjust the way our laws are exercised, all of this supports our economy, which means our program of living. White people and colored. All people serve each other because we are all God's people. Our religion teaches that man is born equal. Black people in the sight of God are the same."

Then, he said: "Now do you feel better? I am going to make some suggestions for you that I think will help. First —don't become bitter toward the white children because of what has happened today. You know you are liked by every body here. You grew up among the people in these ten blocks. You are like any other child in Sewanee to most people. This word Negro should not have come to you the way it came. That is why it is so hard for you to understand. I don't think you have had any association with colored children. So I think it would be best if you would go out of the corporation to where they live and play with them. This will help you in many ways. You will see they are very happy and lovable people. There is nothing bad about being a Negro."

Then, he said: "Is there anything you don't understand now? If so, ask me." By this time I had stop crying, and was listening to every word he was saying. There were many things turning over in my mind going back to my mother by birth. Things she had told me. What she wanted me to be. As young as I were, it seemed to me a Negro was just worthless. What could he be? Still a slave? There was one thing on my mind I just could not get off it—the military academy. I said: "Father, will I go to the military academy when I grow up?" He place his hand on my shoulder, and said: "No, Ely, colored people don't go to school with white people in the South."

This to me was about the hardest blow that I could experience. This was the greatest dream of all the boys I had known. For four years this had been my dream—that some day I would be a cadet. It seemed that everything of hope just floated out of me, and I was just a shell.

Time had passed so fast I did not realize it. Father said: "It is time for tea. It is five o'clock. You had better be going before it is dark." He said: "Ely, you can come to me anytime you want to talk to me. Since you do understand better I want to see that smile on your face again that has made everyone love you. You have been the most happy little fellow I have known. Love everybody now. Your job is making everybody love you. Come to see me more often."

22

I picked my cap up off the floor and walked to the door. Just then I realized I felt close to Father. It seemed that he was helping me so much in so many ways. I had found a friend different than anyone except my mother by birth. I bade him goodbye and started home.

CHAPTER

3

When I got to Dr. Barton's my foster mother was serving
dinner. She gave me a scolding, and ask where I had been.
I told her to Father Eastern's house to talk to him. She said:
"If you don't stop annoying people about being a Negro I
will whip the life out you." She said Frank had told her I
had been crying around the stable that day and asking him
what a nigger was. "Stop asking people questions, especially like that. If I hear of you doing it again I am going
whip you. We are all nigger and there is nothing wrong
about it."

I refused to eat. I tried to tell her what had happened
that day. She didn't seem to care. She didn't want to hear
about it. By this time I was weeping. She was hurrying to
get through with the dishes. I was drying them.

Mrs. Barton came out and congratulated her on the
dinner. She saw that I was crying. She was the most kind
lady. She ask me what was I crying about. Mother spoke,
"He is just about to drive us crazy about him being Negro.
He was called nigger by a clerk at the drugstore a few days
ago, and he thinks it is a disgrace to be a Negro. He has
been around you white people all his life. For that reason
he thinks he should be white." Mrs. Barton smiled at my

mother, and said: "Mattie, don't be too harsh with him. Try to bear with him. It could be more than what you are thinking of. He doesn't know much about colored people. That clerk shouldn't have spoken as he did. Not at that time and to the children. Give him time and he will work it out for himself." She smiled and said good night.

Mother said: "We are going home tonight. Take this pan of food to the room." I went out to the servant room. Soon she came in. While she was changing her clothes she ask me what did Father say. She seem to be different a bit. I was surprised to hear her say: "Ely, I love you as my own. I suppose I just don't understand you. Things will be alright. Don't worry about it." I told her that Father said I should play with colored children some. It would be better for me to know them. I ask if I could stay home the next day and go to play with the colored children. She said yes. We did not talk on the way home.

Mother told her daughter that I was to stay with her tomorrow, and could go to play with the children in the bottom. That was what they called the play ground. I went to bed early.

The next morning my adopted sister Ann talked with me, telling me how to get along with colored people. Her father was a white man and she was often resented by colored people. We talk all morning. I was most fond of her. She taught dancing to both white and colored. She went to homes in neiboring towns. At twelve oclock four white girls came from the poor white side of town. These people were often called the Sagers. That was what the aristocrats and colored called them.

My sister sent me to the playground. When I got there

the kids were playing in groups. The larger boys were playing football. I found that I was in a split group—too young for one, too old for the other. The fifteen year to twelve played football. They would not let me play with them. The others were around seven and eight. I was ten years old.

I stood and looked at the big boys play for awhile hoping that I might be accepted in. When the ball was kicked out of bounds I ran it down and rushed back with it. One of them said: "Throw it here, Clabber." He turned and said to the other boys: "That's Clabber Doane's nephew. He will never have sense enough to play football, and he thinks he is white." I walked away because I hadn't heard the word Clabber for three years—not since I stop school. They all laughed.

I walked across the playground where the younger group around seven or eight were playing. I stood watching them. They were playing a game I hadn't seen before. They called it hop-scotch. I decided to join in with them.

Up walk a big black woman with a bonnet on, and a snuff brush in her mouth. She spoke to two of the children, telling them to come home. She stood staring at me for two or three minutes. I spoke to her saying: "Howdy." She said: "You know, you are sure a bastard if there ever was one."

Up came a young girl around eighteen. Stopped by her side. She said: "Who is that little boy? He's a pretty boy." Then, the big woman turned, and said: "Did you ever see a bastard that wasn't good looking? They are love babies. But who wants one?"

They turned and walked away, and all the children

follow. There was three words I just couldn't bear to be called: Bastard, Clabber, Nigger. I knew there was no point to talk to anyone about it. Who cared? This day was the first time I realized I was an orphan, and that's all. No one really wanted me. Father had told me to love everybody. This I would try to do.

I found myself wishing that God hadn't taken my mother. This last year I had wished much for her.

As I was walking back home I met my grandfather driving his slop wagon home. He lived a half mile out in the forest where he had a hog ranch. He had three barrels full of swill that he collected every day from the boarding houses to feed the hogs. I hadn't seen him very much since my mother died.

He stop to talk to me. Why was I not with Mother Mat? I told him Father Eastern had told me to play with the colored children. He nodded his head. I ask him could I go home with him for awhile. He reached down, caught my hand and pulled me up beside him. He said: "Now, don't worry me with a lot of questions."

He drove on. I sat there silent, much disappointed because I meant to tell him some of what happened that day. I knew he didn't want to hear anything I had to say. The horses plodded along with the heavy load into the woods. Once in awhile he would mumble something to himself.

Soon we reached the feeding pens where he would transfer the slop to other barrels. When this was done he gave a loud hoop hog call. Almost from nowhere hogs came running. Chickens, turkey—all came. He poured the slop in the gutters. The pens were full of hogs, all sizes.

I spoke for the first time, asking him how many hogs

did he have. He didn't answer at once. He stood looking at them eat. I thought he had forgot my question, which I would not ask again. He looked at me for a moment, then said: "I don't know how many hogs I got. I just can't count them. I want you to count them for me." I was glad to hear him ask me.

I leaped off the wagon, climbed up on the board fence, and started to count. When I finished, he was down on his knees in a small pen holding some chicken intestines in his hand. I rushed over to the pen. He had a possum in a box, fatting. I told him he had eighty seven head. He mumbled a bit, shut the lid on the possum, and stood looking at the hogs. I could see he was pleased. He ask me how close was that to a hundred. I told him fifteen. He just grunted several times as he drove to the barn about five hundred yards away. He unhitched the horses. He seemed to be glad to have me along.

He lived alone in a two room log cabin. He had a five acre farm under cultivation, seven cows, one bull. This was the first time I had been to his house in almost three years. He had accumulated much since then. We went into the house.

The fire place still had embers alive. He put on the coffee pot. He brought under his arm something wrapped. It was some food from Miss Emma Tucker's boarding house. Miss Emma always gave colored people food that was left. Grandpa always went there after the noonmeal to pantote whatever was left. Miss Emma's cook was Aunt Harriet Smith and was known throughout the South.

The food was soon hot in the pan—candied sweet potatoes, macaroni, squash, biscuits, fried chicken, cobler. I was hungry. Grandpa and I ate all of it. He remarked what a wonderful woman Mrs. Tucker was. She was such a Christian who loved her servants and helped them everyway she could. He said: "She asks about you every time she sees me. You must stop and see her sometime. You know she raised Lee, your stepfather, and George Price, her headwaiter, who has been with her twenty years. These Sewanee people are the finest in the world. They have sure been good to me."

I asked Grandpa: "Hadn't I better be going? It will soon be dark." He said: "No, wait until I milk the cows. I have to deliver milk to five places, then I will drop you off at Mat's house. I want you to do something before you go." We were sitting on the floor in front of the fireplace, eating off the hearth which he often liked to do.

He went to the kitchen, got the milk buckets, came back and set them by me. Then, he went to the corner of the bedroom, pulled out a small trunk, placed it in front of the fireplace, threw some wood on the fire to make light, and open the trunk. He lifted out some magazines. He said: "While I am milking I want you to count the money in this trunk. It is all silver. I don't like bills. I will close the door. If anyone come, shut the trunk, and don't tell them of the money."

He went out. I started to count, and when he finished milking and came back in, I was still counting. When he finished straining the milk and bottling it I was finished too. He had nine hundred twenty eight dollars and twenty cents, all in silver. I told him the amount. He looked at the money, all in ten dollar stacks. He reached out his hand, and patted me on the head. He said: "Your mama said you would make a smart man someday. Now we know how much is there. Don't tell anybody about it. Remember that —nobody. When I get money I always get silver, and just put it in that trunk. I don't like banks, and I don't want to be robbed." He picked the trunk up and put it back in the corner of the room.

It was dark now. The fire flames were flickering bright as we stood before the fireplace. This was the first time I had seen him a bit happy. I did not ask one question. I remembered Father Eastern told me that when he ask grandpa why he didn't spend some time with me, he said I ask too many questions about things he didn't know the answers to, and I was too much bother.

He covered the trunk with some rags and clothes, but he held out one book that he called his accounts. He knelt in front of the fireplace, opening the book, and began drawing milk bottles on the lines. When he finished drawing on four different pages, he said: "I keep my own books. You see this is the Barnwells, the McCraddys, Tuckers, Johnsons. I deliver milk every evening and morning. I draw all the bottles of milk for a week. Then I collect. When you come back again I want you to help me check up on my customers I do privy work for. They all owe me money from way back." I told him I would be back and would stay some nights.

We came out of the house, and closed the door that didn't have a lock at all. We hitched up the horse to the sulky he used to deliver milk in.

For the last two weeks with colored people I had learned to listen to what they had to say and ask nothing. As a child you were better liked. All white people seemed

30

to like to be asked questions and enjoyed answering them—even the school students that I would talk to that knew me. As John, Grandpa's horse, went winding on the trail through the woods, it was black dark, and I ask, "How could the horse see his way so good and we could not?" He said: "They have night eyes and we don't. Don't start asking questions. You have been a good boy today. You have been a lot of help to me. You will soon be old enough to milk the cows and feed the stock. Then I want you to come live with me. I am going to marry this spring. I am going to buy a rubber tire buggy like the white people have." He said: "I will be rich someday, and you will be just like me. Not afraid of nothing. That's what is wrong with the niggers. They are too afraid. You are my boy, and you are a chip off the old block, ain't you?"

I was feeling happy now, for the first time, to think of being a nigger, and by all means I would be brave. Not afraid of anything. I said: "Grandpa, I think I will start to school soon. Then, I will be so I can help you with your accounts." He answered quickly, saying: "School don't mean anything to a nigger. What do they have to do except work like hell from morning till night year in and year out, and do what the white man tells them to do, and it don't take no education to do that. You be like me. Make your own job. Get something of your own. Don't have no boss. Be on your own. When we niggers come to learn that, then we will be somebody."

The horse had stopped at a small brook where he liked to drink spring water. "You must learn to do for yourself. When I was a boy your age I was a slave. I was put on the block and sold with five other brothers and sisters. My sisters I haven't ever heard of since that day. I haven't been inside of a schoolhouse in my life. That's why I don't like no banks to keep my money. Where I have to ask someone how much I got. And I can't write my own name, so I don't write checks. Money is all a man needs. Just have it. That's what counts. You see, son, nobody tells old Ned what to do. They ask him, will he do what they want him to do? I make my own price. When they want their privies cleaned, slop hauled, trash moved—they ask me, and what is my price? I tell them. Now you see why I got more money than any nigger in Sewanee, except Marcus Handley, who owns the barber shop."

By this time we were at my foster mother's house. He said: "Tell Mat that I kept you late. But don't tell about my money and where I keep it. Come and see me soon. We will go possum hunting next week." I said goodbye, and he drove away. I went into the house.

My sister Ann and her boyfriend was standing before the fire. She ask where I had been. I told her. She kissed me on the forehead, and said: "I've looked for you everywhere. I thought you had gone to Mama at the Bartons. How did you like the kids you played with today?" I told her I didn't play. I was called a bastard, and no one wanted to play with me. Also the big woman said that Clabber Doane was my uncle, and I was crazy like him. I met Grandpa Ned and rode home with him. I am glad I went because he is glad he is a nigger. He told about being a slave when he was a boy and what a man he is. No one bosses him. He has his own job and is not afraid of anybody. Sis smiled, and said: "Was he drunk?" I knew he often got drunk. I said: "No, we had a good time." Jake, her boyfriend, said: "I will be going." I was glad to see him go.

I wanted to talk to Ann. She loved me and I loved her. She was the only one of the family that ever taken time to talk to me. I knew she wouldn't discuss the word Negro. Mama Mat had told her not to talk about it with me. She stood there looking so beautiful, smiling at me as if she was the happiest woman in the world. Then, she said: "To your cheeks, rosy little boy, you are a pretty boy. I am going to let you in on a secret. I am going to marry. Jake proposed to me this afternoon. We will ask Mama tonight to let us marry. Don't tell anyone."

I screamed: "No, Annie, please don't leave me." I ran to her, siezing her around the waist, sobbing, telling her how much I love her, and that she was the only person that love me. "I am called bastard by every body. I want you to tell me what a bastard is." She held me back from her looking down into my eyes with a frown on her forehead. She said, softly: "Tell me who called you bastard." I told her about the big black woman with the bonnet on. How she called me a white bastard.

Ann held me close to her breast, and said: "You poor child, as soon as you get over one hurt you find another. I am not going to leave you. When Jake and I marry we will get a house and you can live with us." I still ask: "Annie, why do I have to be a bastard, and why are bastards not like by colored people?" She kissed me again on my forehead, and pushed me backward into the chair, and said: "Sit there."

She started to hum the tune she knew I like—'Bill Bailey, won't you come?' She two-stepped across the room and back. She said: "Is there anything wrong with me?" I said: "No, Ann, you are beautiful." She said: "I am called a bastard, but it don't worry me now like it use to. Negroes like to hurt people when they can. Some do. They don't know any better. My father is a white man and yours is a white man. That's why we are so white and look different than other Negroes. We have to take many insults. That's why Mama moved to Sewanee from Winchester. Because it was so hard for me there where I was born. I just hated to go to school. The children picked on me so. I use to have a fight every day. But don't fight unless you have to. Try to love everybody." Standing there as beautiful as she was no one would know she was a Negro unless someone told them. I ask her: "Was my cousin Trudy a bastard, too?" She said: "Yes, any child borned out of wedlock is called a bastard."

Some one knocked at the door. There were three musicions who went serenading among the white homes at night. They often stopped at our house to practice awhile before going out to serenade. They played. She made me dance with her a bit. Soon Mama came. The musicions left. Then Jake came back. I was sent upstairs to bed.

This had been an important day for me. I was more at ease than I had been for months. It wasn't so bad to be a Negro if Negroes liked you, so they must like me. I would make them like me. I said my prayers and went to bed.

Next morning, when I came downstairs, everybody was gone except Ann. She was sitting up in bed, sobbing and snuffing her nose. Her eyes were red. I knew she had been crying.

I went to the bed and ask her what was wrong. She said: "Mama don't want me to marry Jake. I am going to marry him if I have to run away. My father wants me to go up north to a school where all white people go. He don't want me to marry just now. He don't want me to marry a Negro. I love Jake, and no one is going to stop us—nobody." She threw the cover back and slid out of bed, putting on her kimono. She said: "I'll fix us some breakfast."

After breakfast she told me I could go to play with the children again. I went back to the playground. There were lots of children there. No one ask me to play. I stood around for hours waiting. The smaller children seemed to be shy of me.

I decided I would go to see Father Eastern, and get the fifty cents he gave me once a month. When I arrived Father was walking to and fro on the yard walk. I yelled out like I used to: "Hello, Father." He raised his hand as a greeting. He said: "You sound like my boy Ely." I walked up to him. I was thinking what grandpa had said: "Don't have fear of anybody." Father caught my hand, and we walked into the house.

He said: "I was just talking to Ned this noon. He told about your visit with him yesterday. He said you didn't ask questions like you used to. He was very glad of that. You should go and see him more often." I ask: "Father, why don't Negroes like to ask questions? You said anything I wanted to know, ask someone that knew. That was the way to learn. You never complain, Father." He did not answer —just smiled. Then, he said: "Did you enjoy playing with the colored children?" I spoke up quickly: "No, Father, they won't play with me. I was called a bastard. A woman and the children just don't care to have anything to do with me." He spoke, saying: "You know, Ned said you are understanding that being a Negro isn't bad at all. I am so glad you do understand."

35

I said: "Father, Grandpa said he was a nigger and was proud of it. So, if he is my grandpa I am going to be just like him. I am not going to be afraid of anybody either. That's the kind of man he is." Father changed the conversation: "Ely, the colored school will be opening in another month and you must go. All the colleges will close December the fifteenth. Then, the colored will open. John Kennerly, who does janitor work now, will be free to teach the school. We don't have another colored person that is qualified as a teacher here. You must go to Sunday school every Sunday beginning Sunday. I will tell Mat to do this. Father Claiborne will be your teacher next Sunday and I will be there too."

He reached over on the table, picked up a small book, and handed it to me. "This is your catechism to keep with you at all times. You must read it. You must love everybody and be happy, and come to see me as often as you might like."

I ask: "Father, can I get fifty cents, please." He said: "Yes, you are just about due it." I planned that the next morning I would go to the store and buy some lemon drops with this money. I would take the candy and give it to the children. Then they would like me better and would be glad to play with me.

As I walked home I thought that this being a Negro wasn't so bad if only this being a bastard could be forgotten. The Negroes have just got to like me, then I will be happy. Just happy. I ran almost all the way home.

Ann and Jake were talking. She pulled me beside her, and said: "Jake, Ely will live with us. He loves me so much." Jake said: "Yes, he will be company for you."

36

Then, he said: "I must be going. It will be time to serve dinner." Ann stood, and kissed him goodbye.

This was the first time I had seen her kiss any man. She was tall, white as could be, with deep blue eyes, gingerbread color hair dropping to her waist, profile like an English lady, beautiful limbs, small hands and feet. Her shoes were number three and one-half. She looked so much like Lillian Russell. Jake was fully six feet tall, black as the skin of anyone could be, and as handsome as could be. He was smiling as he said goodbye. His teeth were white as pearls as if a sculptor had carved them in his mouth. His shoulders were broad and square. He was all man, all hundred and ninety pounds of him. Like all trained servants in Sewanee, I hadn't ever seen him without his collar and tie. All servants that worked in the corporation were always dressed.

When he went out Ann stood looking at the door. This was the first time I had seen a woman stimulated by someone. I really felt I was a part of them. I said: "Ann, Jake is a Negro, but he is not a bastard, is he?" She looked at me. The soft light from the fireplace made her aglow. Her cheeks were flush, her thin lips were so red. She put her arms around me, and said: "My pretty boy, No, he isn't." She bent down and put the side of her face against mine. "You know that woman said bastards are all pretty. Let's dance. I am going to make you my dancing partner." She swung me around a few times.

She said: "Let's have dinner. We have sourbelly, black-eyed peas, and apple pie, which I will cook special for you." She rolled her hair up on her head, and went into the kitchen.

When dinner was over in came the serenaders and be-

37

gan to play. This was my first lesson on dancing. Soon several men had come to see Ann. She was most popular with men. She danced with all of them.

Mama came. She wasn't in a good humor at all. She had business to talk to Ann. Everybody left. She said to Ann: "I have a job for you, and you are going to take it. You will have a chance to go to some big cities and see something, instead of marrying some dumb nigger here. This lady wants you to be her maid, and go with her when she travels. She will be here to see you tomorrow. You will be able to see the world and learn something, too. There is a letter from your white daddy. He don't want you to marry no black Negro. He said he would send you up north to any training school you want to go to. The white people here thinks you should wait awhile and not marry now. You are just like all young girls—boycrazy—so get it off your mind."

All the children listened when Mama spoke. Ann said: "Alright, Mama." I was told to go to bed. I put on my flannel gown, knelt, putting my head against Ann's knees, and said my prayers. Then, I went upstairs to bed, wondering why they didn't like Jake. "He's a nigger and he's not bastard." I remembered that Father said all Negroes were the same, no matter how black or how white. Early in my youth I had come to admire strong physical men like my stepfather was. I was wishing that I was a strong, big, black man like Jake. Ann loved him. I did, too. I thought of my plans for tomorrow, and how I would make all the children like me. I went to sleep.

CHAPTER

4

Next morning Ann and I were alone. She said: "I will teach you to ask the blessing." I told her I knew. I said: "Man that is born of a woman is in this world a few days, and his heart is filled with trouble." When I looked up she was looking strait at me, frowning. "Where did you hear a blessing like that?" I told her that was what Grandpa Ned said the other day when we started to eat. She said: "Uncle Ned gets everything backward. They say that at burial. I want you to listen Ely, to what I have to say. Don't use the word bastard any more. The word nigger either. It is not nice for children to use those words. When anyone call you those words just say, Don't you wish you were goodlooking." She smiled and kissed my forehead.

For the first time I ask her if I could go to the store in the village. I wanted to buy some candy to give to the children at the playground. She said: "Yes, that will be nice."

Someone called from the front gate—a coachman asking for Ann. We both went to the gate. Lady Alton and her husband got out. Lady Alton said: "I know we will like you. You are very pretty. Is this boy your brother, Ann?" Ann said: "No, Madam he is a boy Father Gerry ask Mother Mat to raise. His name is Ely." The lady said: "Oh, I know. He is Lena's boy."

Ann told me to go and play, but not to stay too late. I went to the village to buy candy at John Rupp's store. I bought lemon drops, two pounds for fifty cents.

Then I went to the playground. There were many children that I hadn't seen before. I walked up and set the bag down on the grass, asking everybody to have some candy. They stood and looked at each other. I taken the bag, and passed it to everyone. Some taken a handful. Some refused, especially the ones that had been there a few days before. Two bigger boys came up. One said: "What you got in that bag, Clabber?" They taken the candy, and started away with it. I ran and snatched the bag, throwing the candy all on the ground. Everybody laughed.

I went home to Ann. When I came in the house I was crying. Ann ask me what was wrong. I said: "I don't want to talk." I went up the stairs to my bedroom. Ann came. I was lying across the bed, sobbing. She spoke: "What's wrong, my pretty boy?" I told her that she would not like to hear what happen. "I am just a bastard. Nobody of Negroes like it that way." She said: "Did the children like the candy?" I explained what happen.

She said: "Get up. Put on your sailor suit that Maxwell Noll sent you. I will dress, and we will go to the football game with Georgie Teck. This is a game of the season. Lots of people are here to see this game. Won't that be nice. You haven't ever been to a game." So we decide to go. She said: "If Sewanee varsity beats Georgie, it will be a hot time in Sewanee tonight. We will stay uptown to see the celebration and the barnfire, and come home with Mama when it is over."

She helped me dress. While she was dressing herself

she began telling me about the football team, called the varsity. If they won this game, and beat Vanderbilt on Thanksgiving, they would be the champs of the South. We started to the ballpark a mile away. It looked like most of the colored people was going. We had lots of company along the road. Everybody was boosting for Sewanee. When we got there it looked like everybody in Sewanee was there, colored and white.

We didn't have to pay anything to go in. This was the way the program was for the colored people. Everything of sport and entertainment no colored ever paid. Even the Hospital Clinic was all free.

Soon the teams came on the field. There were no grandstands. The playing field was roped off. Everybody stood and walked to and fro keeping up with the play. Sewanee won 12-6. The people went wild singing and yelling, colored and white. I was happy to think Negroes was some part of white people.

We went to Dr. Barton's and waited until Mama Mat finished her work. By eight o'clock the main street was full of people, colored and white, waiting for the school boys to parade. There was a pile of boxes and rubbish two story high for the barnfire. It burned while the students paraded around it and sang the victory song. It was something to see. It was a hot time in town that night.

We went home. There were many colored going our way. They talking of going to Nashville when the team went to play Vanderbilt on Thanksgiving, if they could have enough money. This was the first time I had heard colored people talking good about white people.

Father Eastern was right: Colored people loved white

41

people. It was very dark. Many had lanterns so we could see how to follow the path through the woods. There were no sidewalks in the town, except on the main streets where poor people did not live. Some of the young men with us stopped at our house and had a glass of wine.

I was soon sent to bed. I lay in bed thinking I would never be like other Negroes. They would not let me be a part of them. The children would never accept me. To be a child of God I would love everybody. I knew tomorrow I would have to go to Sunday School. Would it be like the schoolday when the boys called me Clabber? I knew I had to go.

Next morning, after breakfast, I ask: "Could I go to see the cadets and their band march to church?" Mama said: "Yes." I did not care to be close to the street they were on like I use to do. I just stood two blocks away and watched them march by. What a beautiful sight it was. I said to myself: "It is really something to be a white man."

I looked on as the carriages passed by—men with high plug hats on. My mother's words came back to me, when she use to say: "I want you to be a fine man like that man." I decided I would never be a nigger or a Negro, no matter what my grandfather had said. He was glad he was a nigger. These white men were so neatly dressed, and my grandfather was so dirty and greasy and smelled like slop.

I remembered I was to go to Sunday School that afternoon, so I started home, thinking of my grandfather's words: "Niggers have to work day in and day out, always. Be your own boss. Then you are somebody." That what I will do. I will work. When I thought of Sunday School I hoped the children wouldn't call me a bastard and a clabber at church.

Along came a boy four or five years older than I with a shoe shine box. He had been to some of the boarding houses, shining shoes. I hadn't seen him before that day. He didn't play with the other boys at the playground. He spoke: "You are the boy that Miss Mattie Davis is raising. Your name is Ely." I said: "Yes." As I looked at him, I thought to myself: "He must be the blackest Negro in Sewanee, but I wish I was like him." He talk all of the way home. He was different from the other boys.

I had to pass his house before I got to our house. When we got to his gate, his brother was waiting for him. They looked like the gold-dust twins. The older boy was name Houston, the younger was Simon. He ask me in to have some ice cream. Their mother sold cream every Sunday to children. I went in. Houston told her who I was, and that Father Eastern was my counselman. Her name was Sally Smith. She was as black as she could be, and as kind as she could be. She served me a big saucer of cream.

She looked so much like the woman with the bonnet that had called me a bastard, I was afraid to talk to her at first. When I had finished my cream, I thanked her and told her I must be going because I had to go to Sunday School that afternoon. Houston said: "Simon and I will be going, too. We are Episcopalian. We sing in the choir. Father Eastern will be there this evening. We will stop for you."

I was so happy to think there were Negroes like me. I ran home into the house telling Mama about the wonderful people I had met. This was the first time for quite awhile I had said anything that pleased my Mama. I ask her: "Can I go with them to Sunday School?" She said: "Yes. These are the finest boys in Sewanee and the finest family." This was the beginning of a lifelong friendship.

They came for me. They were so curteous, pulling off their hats and bowing to my Mama. She smiled, which she didn't do too often. They assured her they would take care of me. I tagged along behind them until we got to the church. Father Eastern, Father Claiborne and another Father, a student of theology, were standing out in front of the chapel.

Father Eastern said: "Houston, I am so glad to see you have Ely with you. I would like you to lead him along. He is a fine boy and needs big brothers like you two." Houston answered: "We will be." He and Simon went to the vestibew to put on the carter and gown with the choir. There were many children there. No one seemed to notice me which made me very happy.

When it was over I waited until the boys changed. They came out with Father Eastern and the student Father. We walked home with Father Eastern which was much out of our way. When we reach Father's house he said: "That was a nice visit, boys. See you tonight." He smiled and went in his gate. As we walked home we joined hands. I was between them. We sang as we walked. When I got home I was so happy to tell Ann and Mama how I enjoyed going to Sunday School. For many months I would go on Sunday mornings to Mrs. Sally Smith and help freeze the ice cream. She would let me lick the dasher.

Monday morning I decided I was going to find some work. After breakfast I went out on the street hoping to find something to do. The leaves had fallen in many yards where they didn't have men help. I would ask if I could rake up the leaves. I only looked for the small yards. Most of the homes were like estates, so called now—large houses of ten to fifteen rooms with grounds of two to three acres. Most such homes roomed students.

The first job I got was at Miss Mary Miller's boarding house, and the second was Miss Carey Johnson's home. These were small yards. I charged twenty five cents each yard which taken me three days to finish. These two ladies like me very much. They would send me to the drugstore with notes for whatever they wanted. Soon I could find somebody would give me something to do for a dime or a quarter. This didn't last long because the schools all closed on the fifteenth of December. The vacation period was in the winter months at that time. Over half of the aristocrats went away for the winter because it was bitter cold on the mountains. Even most of the servants went to towns in the low lands.

All of my family stayed at Sewanee, except Ann. Her new job taken her away. She travelled with Lady Alton. She went to Louisville, New Orleans, Nashville, Atlanta, Memphis. For three months Mama and I stayed home. She quilted several quilts. I batted cotton for the quilts.

When it wasn't too cold I would go to see Houston or my brother. I didn't care about playing with other children anymore. Houston and Simon never went to play with the other boys. They stayed at home. They studied books. They had an organ they played. They were always busy. Mrs. Sally taught them to keep busy. When I could be with them I was learning something just like I was when I was with Mother Gerry and her family.

The town was just dead for three months. School would not open until March the fifteenth. The only amusement for the colored was to play cards—a game named

45

five up which was played with partners. They would go from house to house to play.

Gambling was much forbidden in Sewanee. People didn't have much money. Wages was low. The popular wage for adults was ten dollars a month no matter what you done. Your meal was given. No one ever went hungry in Sewanee. The men that done construction got one dollar a day for ten hours. Everybody had credit at the grocers'. If they ran out of money during vacation period they lived on credit until school opened.

Many of the white people who were still in Sewanee would drive around among the colored people asking how they were doing. There was always a doctor you could go to without cost. Medicine could be obtained. If you didn't have money you could charge it until you were able to pay.

Christmas I enjoyed more that year than any I had since my Mother died. I went to the Christmas tree which was given by the church. No one carried presents. Everyone went to get presents—toys, clothes, candy, popcorn, many things that would supply your needs. This was the first time I had seen a Christmas tree. I got many presents—particularly a drum that was a beauty.

It used to be down South that on Christmas people shot fireworks after the tree was over. There was a roman candle battle for the larger boys which was very pretty to see. Many white people came to see we children enjoy ourselves. Father Claiborne blessed us. This was my first happiness for some time. I had forgotten about being a bastard and a Negro. I had friends—not only white people but Negroes, Houston and Simon.

School opened for the colored, but the weather was

so rough Mama did not make me go. I didn't want to go—
it only lasted three months anyway. Prof. Kennerly was
studying to be an Episcopal Father. He taught school and
served as a janitor. He often taught the Sunday School
class. Uncle Calvin Childress played the organ. All by ear.
He had a band which the white people helped by giving
instruments. They played country music. All by ear.

I heard much about what the Negroes done in
Sewanee. They had football teams and baseball teams.
They were coached by the college coach, and were the best
around. Teams would come from all towns to play our
teams. White people would attend the games and contribute to the expense.

In 1905 Fisk University came to play. The colored
people could not accomodate them so the white people
made room in the dormitory for them. This was the real
Sewanee sixty years ago.

When my sister Ann returned from her job and travel
she told of all the things she had seen. How wonderful Mrs.
Alton had been to her. How she had passed for white at
times for better accomodations. How she had combed
her hair with the Lady's comb and brush. How white men
that didn't know she was a Negro had flirted with her.
How she and her Madam had laughed about it. Her Madam
had told her she should go north where her opportunity
would be greater. In New Orleans she won a waltz con-
test. She lost in the cake walk.

Mama and I had been so lonesome for Ann that Mama
gave in that she could marry Jake. The engagment was
announced. It created an interest among many of the
white. They would stop their carrages in front of the house

47

and call Mama out. They would ask her why she let Ann marry a man as black as Jake. All Mama would say was "Are we not all Negroes?" They would shake their heads and drive away. Some of them sent for Ann and tried to talk her out of it. Soon Ann would not talk to them at all. This went on for weeks.

Mama was much unhappy about the way white people were concerned. One night, while she quilting on the frame and sitting by the fireplace, she said: "I don't understand white people. They bring about bastards, and then want to run their lives. Why can't we live our own lives? I've had the same trouble when I was freed of slavery. Now you, and perhaps Ely, will have the same thing. Their sins live with us all our lives. Your father hasn't done anything for you—not like he should have. Now he wants to tell you how to live your life. So, don't pay any attention to anyone. Jake is a good man, and that is that."

Ann rose from her seat, went over to Mama and put her arms around her from behind. They were shedding tears. Ann said: "This means so much to me, Mama."

This was the first time I had seen Mama Mat cry. She was the most stern woman I ever knew. I don't think she was afraid of anything. Her husband had died three years after their marriage, leaving two children, both boys, one six months, the other one and a half years old. She never married again. Two years later Ann was born. Mama Mat worked and raised her own. She had to be a strong woman. She raised my mother, and now she was raising me. That night I knew she was all I could ever wish for as a mother.

The wedding taken place in about two weeks. We had somewhat a party. White people that had protested came in carriages, and brought many presents—almost everything the couple could use for housekeeping—furniture, dishes, cooking utensils. Much of it was used, but it was better than they were able to buy.

Mama moved things out of the house so people could dance. The white people left as soon as the ceremony was over. The colored people danced and partied all night. There was string music. This night no one told me when to go to bed, so I stayed up with the party. Ann and Jake were such a handsome couple.

They left the next morning on the six o'clock train for Winchester, Tennessee, ten miles away, to spend a week's honeymoon in the town where she was raised.

When they returned they decided to live with Mama Mat. We had a happy family.

Soon the schools opened. Sewanee was back out of hibernation. Mama went back to work for Dr. Barton. I stayed with Ann most of the time. Having Houston and his brother to play with, and Ann, I forgot about the Academy boys.

Nothing much changed for two years for me. I would see Father Eastern at Sunday School.

The next year Ann gave birth to a boy. A few weeks later our house burned. We lost almost everything we had. All my happiness faded out. We had to move across town where there were no children at all. I was then around twelve years old.

Houses were scarce. Mrs. Weber, a white lady, let us live in a house in the back of her estate. We were given almost everything we had lost in the fire. This is the way white people treated the Negroes then.

Mama taken rhumatism badly and had to stop cooking. She and Ann started doing hand laundry. This kept me most busy. I had to look after her son, and carry water from the well to wash with. I didn't see any children— only on Sunday when I went to Sunday School. They bought me a wagon so I could deliver clothes. I was not loved like I had been. Soon no one ever thought of me except when they need me to do something.

I became to be stubborn. I was whipped, often for the least thing. Past unpleasantness came back in my mind. I started resenting again that I was a Negro. I would alway know I was a bastard and an orphan.

I was given a dog named Tepsy. This was the only friend I felt I had. I would run away into the woods and stay for hours—just me and my dog. Often I would sit and tell him my troubles. It seemed he understood. Then, I would return home to take my whipping. This lasted almost two years.

CHAPTER
5

One morning a man rode up to our gate on a sorrel horse. I called Mama to the door. She yelled at Thomas: "What are you doing here?" He came in and hug Mama and Ann. He said: "Just rode over here from Bridgeport, Alabama, to see you, Mat."

He told her he would like her to come and keep house for him. "I am your cousin. I am now all alone. My girls have married and moved away. I have a good business. My livery stable is doing good. I need someone to keep house for me. You know how I will treat you. Just like I did twelve years ago when you came. Think it over."

Mama fixed him breakfast while he unsaddled his horse. I said: "Mama, take me with you." I was holding her grandson on my lap. She said to the baby: "I only hate to leave you." She loved him so much. I did, too, only he taken all my time nursing him. If anything happened to him that caused him to cry I was whipped.

Uncle Tom came in and sat down for breakfast. She showed him the baby. Uncle Tom said: "Mat, you will come to me, and try it. It's not like it was before when you had three children and I had two. You don't have anyone. So if you don't like it I will send you back anytime."

Mama began to serve the breakfast—sausage, grits, fried apples and buttermilk biscuits. Uncle Tom sat for a minute looking at the food. Then said: "Mat, you can't write and I can't either, so I rode sixty miles over the mountains to see you face to face, and explain how bad I need you. I haven't had a meal like this in years. Over there you will have a horse and buggy anytime you want it. You have your Baptist church to attend which you don't have here. This white peoples' religion is nothing. You can have anything you want."

Mama was holding her grandson, feeding him bites of apple. I saw—for the second time—tears falling on her cheeks. "How long will you stay?" He said: "I am going to Winchester tomorrow to see Grant. I will be there one day, then I will start back to Bridgeport."

Mamma said: "Jake is going to Texas to try a job that will pay him sixty dollars a month." Uncle Tom said: "That is some wages—more than fifteen dollars a month."

Mama said: "Tom, there is something you don't know about. That boy sitting by you I have agreed to raise. He is Ned Green's grandson. I promised Lena, his mother, before she died that I would raise him. I will have to take him with me. This may be a good thing for him. He has the same trouble, his father being white, that Ann had in Winchester when she was small. That's why I came to you the last time." Uncle Tom said: "Bring him. I forgot to tell you about a boy I take care of. His mother died and left him. I just couldn't see the boy go to an orphan home. So I taken him. He's a couple of years older than this boy. They will make a good team."

Mama said; "He can go to school, too. I will have to

52

talk to the white people about this. His Godfather is Bishop Gailor. Mrs. Dr. Richerson is his Godmother. His father is one of the highest family of the town. They promised to help me with him. It's been very little so far. Now I think I will go to them."

Uncle Tom said: "Mat, I wouldn't worry about that. White people don't do anything for their bastards. That is the same condition with this boy I have. His father is a Jew who has a clothing store in Bridgeport. He taken advantage of the boy's mother when she was sixteen. After he was born the girl turned to be a sporting woman and died ten years later. The child lived from house to house. He loved horses so he hung around the stable trying to be of help. He liked me so I adopted him. His father has never give him one dime. You know what I think of white people. They are no good. That's why I don't work for them."

I was proud of Uncle Tom. He was like Grandpa Ned. I had to butt in: "Uncle Tom, can I take my dog with me?" He put his hand in his pocket, pulled out a dollar, and said: "This is his fare to Alabama." Mama said: "It will be at least three weeks, Tom, before I will be there. We are going to move next week over where the Negroes live in the bottom. We can get the Pete Ferris house."

I was told to go to the spring and get fresh water, which I had to do three times a day. When I got back Uncle Tom was asleep. Ann and Mama had started ironing the wash. I had to deliver some laundry to the Gillem home.

It came to me: "In Bridgeport I won't have to nurse children, and won't have to carry water to fill barrels. I won't be call bastard nor clabber. I will go to school. I can be like my Uncle Tom and Grandpa Ned. They like to be Negroes. I am going to be like them. I will be a man when I come back and will beat up any one that calls me names. I won't be afraid of no one."

I reached the Gillem home. As I started up the drive I met Mrs. Gillem in her carriage. She stop as I pulled my wagon off to the side. She spoke: "You have the laundry from Mat. You are Ely. Here is the money, seventy five cents. Put it in your pocket, and don't lose it. Take the clothes to the back door and call Lisa. She will take them. We are late for the party at the McCradys."

There beside her sat a Negro woman dressed in white. Mrs. Gillem said: "Mamy, we had better be going." They drove away. I left the laundry and went home. I was wondering if the Negro woman could be the white woman's mother. She called her Mamy, and they are going to a party. I rushed home. I would ask a question even if it caused a whipping.

I handed Mama the money, and said: "Mama, please let me ask a question." Uncle Tom said: "What is it?" "Is Mrs. Gillem's mother a Negro? She was riding with an old Negro with hair as white as cotton. Mrs. Gillem called her 'Mamy,' and said they were going to a party. I just had to ask you." All three looked at each other. Ann was smiling.

Uncle Tom said: "There is nothing wrong with asking what you don't know." Mama said: "No, that is not her mother by birth. Her name is Clara. She raised Mrs. Gillem from a baby. Mrs. Gillem's mother died with childbirth. Mamy Clara wet-nursed her, and has been beside her all her life. This is called the black Mamy. Some white people

54

think it honorable to keep them around. She taken her to teas and parties with her."

Uncle Tom said: "Son, it's like this in the South. A Negro is a 'boy' until he is a man. Then, he is a 'Dad' or an 'Uncle.' Women are 'Aunts' or 'Mamys.' This is the white man and his law. 'Uncles' and 'Mamys' they carry around with them. They try to square themselves with God for the way they have worked them half to death." He spoke with assurance as if he knew what he was talking about.

He said: "Mat, I am riding to Winchester now. Will see you all tomorrow night."

That night Jake came home most glad. He had a money order for one hundred dollars that a white friend had sent for train fare to Waxahachie, Texas, where he would report for work in ten days at Trinity University, an Episcopal coed school. He said: "I will leave in three days. I have already told Mrs. Vaness about it."

Next morning we started packing things for moving. My job was catching all the chickens and pigs, which was fun for me and my dog. In two days we were all settled. I found my job much harder. I had to carry water twice as far. I had to carry clothes to and fro much farther. I had to stay busy all day, every day.

Jake left for Texas. Ann was alone with her small son. Mama Mat decided it would be better to leave me with Ann for awhile. She went to Alabama alone and would send for me later. I would go to her at Christmas, which was five weeks away.

I was back around the colored people I had tried to be friends with three years ago. We lived two hundred yards from the playground where the colored children played, although I didn't care to play. In fact, I did not have time to play.

Ann was a fine laundry woman. She had all the work she could do, working from ten to fifteen hours a day. Since Mama left my work had doubled. I had to clean house, wash dishes, help with Ann's son, and do most of the delivery. The only time I had any enjoyment was on Sunday when I went to Sunday School. No one called me a bastard or clabber at Sunday School. This was why I enjoyed it so much. All the Fathers were so kind to me.

Ann became to be more like she was when I first came to them. She often went with me carrying the delivery. I found out she was trying to make money to go to Texas. I wanted to help all I could.

One morning a man name Mr. Rosborough rode up to the gate on his horse, and called for Ann. He had a small package of laundry to be done as a special favor for his wife which would be needed by noon the next day. He said: "Ann, you know you and Mat are the best wash women in this town. My wife Sarah thinks so. I am sorry that you people are going away to Texas. Jake, I know, has already gone. Mat has gone to Alabama. That leaves you and Ely alone. Now don't let any thing worry you. If you should need me just let me know. When Ely grows up I want him to be my butler."

He said good bye and rode away. We stood watching his beautiful horse striding down the road. Ann said: "He is the most handsome man in Sewanee. I have heard that he is a Jew. I can't help what he is. He sure is good to colored people."

Next morning at seven o'clock Ann gave me the package to take to Mrs. Rosborough. She told me to rush because these were two blouses Mrs. Rosborough would take to Nashville to wear. I had to go a good mile from where we lived in to the corporation.

I hadn't seen Mrs. Rosborough for two years. She and her husband were younger than most people that kept a home in the corporation. She was a beautiful woman. When I entered with the laundry she spoke kindly, saying how nice Ann was to do this odd job for her. She gave me ·a half dollar as a tip, saying: "This is for getting here early. When you grow up you will be my house man, and I will teach you everything in a training." I was very happy. This was the first time anyone had ever given me a half dollar as a tip.

How large the grounds were where these people lived. Their yards were from one acre to five. There were few streets that was straight for more than five blocks. The streets were like trails meandering around the estates. There were no objections to trespassing through the estate. I decided to cut down my walking by going through yards.

I went through Mrs. Tucker's yard. She had the biggest boarding house in Sewanee. She was buying turkeys that was already dressed from a peddlar who supply many of the homes with poultry and dairy products. His name was Crownover. I stop to look at the turkeys. I hadn't seen turkeys sold dressed before.

Mrs. Tucker was figuring the amount to write the check. As she turned to go in the house she saw me. I pulled off my cap and bowed to her. She said: "Ely, you are sure

growing up. I heard you had gone to Alabama with Mat."
I explained that I was going later. Then, I said: "I haven't
seen turkeys sold like that." She said: "It's good to
buy them that way. Tomorrow is Thanksgiving Day. All
of the students have gone to Nashville for the Vanderbilt
game. There are very few boarders left here for Thanksgiving dinner, so I want as many of the servants as I know
to come and have dinner here. Would you like to come?"
I thanked her, assuring her I would.

I had to pass Father Eastern's house. I stopped in for a
minute to tell him about going to Alabama. He was sitting
by the window, facing the street. He beckoned me with
his hand to come on in. I opened the door and went in the
study where he was writing. I explained to him that I was
going away. He said: "I know. Mat talked to Father Gerry.
It's alright. Mat thinks it will be good for you, the change.
You can go to school, also. I want you to be a good boy,
study hard, go to church and Sunday school. You haven't
missed a Sunday going to Sunday school since you started
three years ago. That's a good record for you. Write me
once and a while. I do want to know about you."

I ran most of the way home. I knew I had lost a bit of
time. Ann would be angry. When I got home I rushed
into the house. Ann wanted to know what kept me so long.
I gave her the dollar the lady gave me for her. Ann was
surprised to get a dollar for just two blouses, even if the
collar and cuff trimmings were pleated. She forgot all
about me being late.

I told her that Mrs. Emma Tucker told me to come to
Thanksgiving dinner. "Can I go?" She smiled, and said:
"Yes, little Negro boy. About the only way you will eat

58

turkey will be at some white peoples' house. Turkey is much too rich for Negro blood."

Ann continued talking, as she ironed, about Mrs. Emma Tucker. "She is such a Christian lady, always treating colored people nice. And her three daughter are the same way. She was good to Lena, your mother, when she was sick. Often she sent food to her, tasty food that she thought she would enjoy. I love her so much. She and many of these ladies helped me get nursing jobs when I was a young girl. She is just sweet."

She said: "You carry the water today. And tomorrow you can have the whole day to do what you would like, because we are going to be busy this next two weeks. I am going to get Grace Childress to help do the washing. The schools all close in two weeks. Lots of ladies will want quick laundry done. There will be dances and parties a plenty. You will have lots of delivery. This is fast money. You see, my boy, I am depending on you."

I was so happy to think that I meant so much to her. I carried water and filled the two barrels by five o'clock. Ann said: "Little boy, when I finish ironing this piece, we will have to go to the store and do some shopping. You need some clothes." I didn't have but two pair of pants, and they had been patched so much they were almost quilted.

We went to the village to Mr. Winn's store. Ann's son was large enough for me to carry him on my back. We taken him along. She bought me a pair of patent leather shoes, a cap, a pair of pants with bows at the knees, which all cost four dollars. I was now dressed up. I was so proud and happy.

Next morning I helped her with the dishes. When we

were through, I dressed and went on my way. I stopped at Mrs. Sally Smith's house to see Houston and Simon. I hadn't been to their house in two years. They were much glad to see me. They ask me to have dinner with them. They were having turkey. Mrs. Sally said: "We raise our turkies." There were many turkies in the yard. This was why they could afford it. I told them I was going to Mrs. Tucker's for dinner. I stayed a half hour and went on.

As I walked along I thought of the Smiths, how they were different from other colored people. We had never had turkey at home. Grandpa raised turkeys. He never ate them. He always sold them to the white people.

When I arrived at Mrs. Tuckers, I was too early. It was twelve thirty. The white folks were eating. We wouldn't eat until they had finished, which would be one thirty. Aunt Harriet told me to go to the servant quarters and see Uncle Peter, her husband. He was very old, too old to do much work. Mrs. Tucker just let him stay around. He had worked for her for many years.

I went in to his room. He was very hard of hearing. When I told him who I was, he chuckled a bit and told me many stories of the past of his life. He liked to talk about slavery, which I did like to hear.

One story I have thought of many times: how the Ku Kluck Klan got started. He said many of the men slaves would slip off and go to other plantations to dance at corn shucking. The next day they would be worn out, not fit for work. Many of the masters had talked ghost stories to the slaves to create fear in them. So, when they would find their slaves had slipped off, they would wrap themselves in white sheets and way-lay them coming home. Then, they would chase after them, which would almost scare them to death. At first it was called Patter Roll. It worked so well on the slaves that it was used on the carpetbaggers after the war. That was when they named themselves K.K.K. It became to be an organization that also created violence. Uncle Peter talked a little, and have his laugh a while, enjoying his own story.

One of the waitresses came to the door and said dinner was ready. He got his cane and we came out to the kitchen where Aunt Harriet was the cook. She told us to go to the table outside on the porch.

There were about fifteen colored people sitting at the table. They were waiting for the maids to bring the food on: My stepfather, my grandfather Ned, Uncle Marcus, who was the barber for the white people. There were seven servants and four other people I didn't know.

Just as the food was put on the table and all was ready to eat, Mrs. Emma Tucker came out to the table. She was smiling as she stood at the end of table. Everybody stood up. She said, smiling: "This makes me so happy to have so many of you young and old here to enjoy what God has given us. Most of you have served me faithfully. I am so grateful to have you come enjoy yourselves." Then, she said: "Uncle Peter, will you bless the food." He did. She went back in the house.

We ate the dinner. The menu was turkey, oyster dressing, corn pudding, the best ever, rice, giblet gravy, English peas, cranberry sauce, plum pudding with brandy sauce. What a dinner! How every one ate! No one could cook like Aunt Harriet.

Just as we finished, there was a commotion in the house. The guests were yelling. Mrs. Tucker came out, and said: "They telephoned from Nashville that Sewanee was leading Vanderbilt at the half 12 to 6." Everybody began to shout—even Uncle Peter and Aunt Harriet. Everyone was excited.

One of the waitresses said to grandpa Ned: "Uncle Ned, won't you do us a spiritual table-walking tonight?" This I hadn't heard of before, that my grandfather could make a table walk. I knew nothing of this. After a few minutes pleading by the girls, he agreed, if there were as many as ten of them. He would do a spiritual interpretation that night at his house. People should come before ten o'clock.

Mrs. Tucker came out again. She said: "It was good that you all came. Some of you are a part of me." She look at me, putting her hand on my shoulder, saying: "This boy's mother was the finest girl that was ever in Sewanee. She served me and everyone so willingly, and, Ely, I do hope you will carry her thoughts." She started back into the house, calling out to Aunt Harriet: "Give what's left to Lee and Ned." Everyone said goodbye.

I said: "Grandpa, can I go home with you?" I had not seen much of him since we moved to the other side of town. I wanted to see the table walk. He said: "I'll be going as soon as I empty these slop cans. But don't ask so many questions. You have been very quiet today. You have acted like a child ought to. Be seen and not heard. You are better liked. Staying around Negroes has helped you a lot."

I noticed Grandpa was just as greasy and dirty as he was the last time I saw him. I rode all the way home with him. He never said one word to me. He mumbled to himself all the time. When we got to the pens, he had to empty the slop. I noticed he had many more cows than he had when I was there last two years before.

When we went into the house, he built the fire up. It was chilly. He had a jug of whiskey, and made a tody for me. He taken a drink right from the jug, and said: "Jack Daniels make the best whiskey in the whole world."

He handed me the broom, saying: "Sweep clean. I am going to clean myself up a bit. Then I am going to teach you how to milk. I have ten cows all giving milk, and all Jerseys." When we finished cleaning I went outside with him.

There was a small tree, a rope hanging from it. He pulled the rope over to him, taking a sack tied to a limb, and said: "This coon should be just right now for cooking." We went back in the house. He taken the animal out. It was all dressed for cooking. I had seen many coons cooked, but this had longer legs than any I had seen. He cut it up and put it in the fire place kettle and swing it over the blaze to cook.

He went out again to milk. He gave me a bucket. He showed me how to squeeze the tit and pull. The cow kicked me and the bucket away. This was the first time I had seen him laugh for a long time. He finished, and said: "I don't deliver milk this evening, because the white people are all in Nashville. So we will take a nap before them gals come to hear the fortune." He strained the milk.

Back in the house he looked at the coon, and said: "Don't he smell good?" He taken another drink of whiskey, went over to the bed and got a pillar, put it on the floor in front of the fireplace and layed down on the floor. He told me that if the pot boiled over to wake him.

I set by the fire, thinking: "How can this man tell fortunes and make a table walk? How different he is from other people. He lives alone. Why don't he get in bed? He must not like me even if I am his grandson. He never comes to see me like he does Eddie Lee, my brother. I am going away. When I come back I will be grown. Then he will want to talk to me. Maybe I won't want to talk to him." I sat there for three hours looking in the fire.

There was a knock on the door. I opened it. A Negro man was standing on the porch. He said: "Would you let me come in and get warm?" I awaken Grandpa. He ask him in.

The man said: "I am on my way to Nashville. I have been working in the mines at Tracy City. I was layed off. We colored people only git to work when it's booming. I was just about to starve. I had to leave that town. I was hoboing my way. They put me off at Mont Eagle, a little town about eight miles from here. Now I am walking my way."

Grandpa got up off the floor, pulled the pot from over the blaze, punched the fork in the coon, and said: "It is done." He hadn't said anything to the man at all. The man was very tall and looked to be almost as old as Grandpa. Grandpa looked at the man, and said: "I am Ned Green. Have a seat. This is my grandson." The man said: "I am Wesley Howard." He sat down. He and Grandpa talked about the hard times Negroes have keeping in work.

Grandpa ask: "Are you hungry?" Wesley said: "I haven't eaten in two days." Grandpa kinder chuckled, and said: "I have a big coon cooked here if you would like

64

it." Wesley said: "Would I like it." Grandpa went to the kitchen for a plate and some milk. I didn't want any. Grandpa didn't eat any either, not just now. Wesley ate the third helping. Grandpa urged him to eat all he could.

It was after nine. The girls would be coming soon. Wesley ask, could Grandpa let him sleep somewhere for the night? Grandpa said: "I have no place to put you. I have only one bed. You can sleep in the barn in the hay if you don't smoke and set the hay afire." Wesley thanked him and went out to the barn, thanking Grandpa for such a good dinner.

Grandpa set there looking amused about something. I was wondering what. He laughed, and said: "You know, this is the first time I ever cooked a fox. I caught him in a trap. He has been stealing my chickens. He was so fat. I knew some one would come along and I would have to feed them. He sure did eat that fox, over half of it. Let's we taste it." I said: "No, sir. They say a fox is a dog, Grandpa, and we are not to eat dogs." He put the lid on the pot, built the fire up bright, changed his clothes, telling me not to be asking questions during the spiritual service. I said I would not.

Soon the girls came—seven girls, three men. There was not enough chairs. Some had to sit on the bed. I had to get on the bed back of them. Grandpa went into the kitchen, brought out the table and put it in the center of the room. He pulled the drawer half out. He said the spirits would grow in the drawer, when they came, not likely before twelve oclock.

We would just sit and think of what we want our spirits to tell us. "If you don't believe in spirits, it will be

65

hard for me to get a message for you sometimes, not often. Don't be scared of sounds. Don't talk, only when I tell you to. We will be silent for a while. Don't go to sleep. You will get sleepy. Keep thinking of who you want to hear from."

The clock was striking eleven. He said: "We will go into the spiritual world. Now, just sit quiet for awhile." He sat down to the table, putting his hands flat on the table with the palms down. There he sat. Everything was so quiet. I layed back on the pillar.

When I awaken the service was over. Everybody was asking him: "What did this mean?" He was telling them: "That is what the spirits said. I don't know what it means." They were standing looking at each other, puzzled at what had happened.

One of the men turned the table over, looking as if he thought it was a trick table. Then he righted it again, and said: "I thought the legs was going to break. It sure did crack and move." I was so disappointed that I went to sleep. I had heard Mama Mat talk about him making the table walk.

It was twelve-thirty now. Everyone left. As we walked home, all they talked about was Grandpa and what the spirits said.

Ann was still up. The baby was not well. I started to tell about my experience at Grandpa's. She said: "I have seen it. He is good."

Next morning, Ann was telling me to get up and go to the village and get six bars of soap. This was wash day. When I got to the store, I learned that Sewanee had beat

Vanderbilt. The eight-thirty train had arrived. The team was in a hand wagon. The students were pulling it with a long rope, about a hundred of them. Everybody was celebrating.

For weeks the colored people that went to Nashville talk of how Sewanee trounced the Commodores. All day Friday and all night, Sewanee celebrated, black and white. I was like the rest. I loved every thing about Sewanee, even if I could not go to school like the white people.

Saturday morning, I taken some laundry to the Vaness house. I met a lady and her son. She was Gertrue Coaly. Her son was named Marland. She was the Vaness cook. While I was waiting for the money, this kind lady, who had brown skin, and was short, and a bit fat, talked to me. She said: "You are Ely, aren't you?" I said: "Yes," slowly, because I never knew what to expect to be said to me—I might be called bastard or clabber. I was always on guard. Not many people had kind things to say to me.

She looked at me for a moment. Then, she said: "I have a boy. You may know him. His name is Marland. I knew your mother. She had big plans for you. Too bad she had to leave you. I have heard that you are a smart boy and a lot of help to your family. It's too bad you don't have some one to send you to school. It would be good if you could go to Winchester where there is a good school. You have an Auntie there, you know. They have a fine school taught by Dr. Towson. I am most proud of my boy. He will graduate at fifteen. He is going to be doctor, when he grow up."

I ask: "Where is your son?" She smiled, and said: "He

is probably talking with some of the white students. They keep him with them most of the time. He enjoys being around them. They think he is very smart."

One of the maids brought me the money. I said: "Good-bye." She said: "Wait, I will give you a piece of cake." A boy came up the steps. He said: "Hello."

I knew I had seen him before talking at the confectionery stand with about fifteen S.M.A. cadets. They had been talking about some man I had never heard of. He told them this man's work hadn't been completed according to the history of Aristotle, Socrates, Plato. I had walked away thinking that a man with such a name had to be somebody. But I wondered how the cadets could have fun with a Negro. I wondered if they called him a nigger.

I didn't know who he was until Mrs. Gertrue came to the porch with my piece of cake. She said: "This is my son." She kissed him on the forehead, asking: "Did you have a pleasant day?" He said: "Yes, Mother." He mentioned the names of some students. "We have been out to Morgan Steep. They are preparing for their exams next week. They say I am a lot of help to them. We will meet there tomorrow and study and debate."

He had a book in his hand which he said he must read that night. It was on English philosophy.

I said good-bye, not thinking that thirty years later this boy and I would come to be close friends two thousand miles away in another state—California—where he became to be one of our finest doctors.

As I walked home, I couldn't help but think how a mother loves her own. She was so proud of him because he was educated. White people like Negroes that are educated. Could I become to be that way? It is something to have people like you. I wondered why he never came over in the bottom where the Negroes play ball. I wondered if he was a bastard. White people seem to like bastards, but Negroes don't. He was light-complected with coarse black hair. He looked like an Indian. Perhaps he was. His mother said she knew my mother.

I decided that afternoon that I was going to be educated regardless of what Grandpa had said. I was in some way going to be educated. I would do as Father Eastern had so many times told me: I would go to school. This I must do. I didn't know how I would do it. I would go to Winchester to this great man Dr. Towson.

When I got home there was another delivery ready. Ann went with me. The wagon was loaded with laundry. We had five different houses to deliver. That was why she went. Also, we had to pick up laundry to bring back. All the ladies were getting ready for the Commencement dance to be held at Frenzy Hall.

The Rosborough home was our last stop. Mrs. Rosborough was delighted to have Ann come herself. She told Ann if she needed anything while her husband was away she should let them know: "We are your friend." I loved her for this kindness so much. We started for home a half mile away. Ann talked much about the fine white friends we had. The Rosboroughs were her favorites.

As we started through the park we met a white man of the sager class—poor white trash as they were called by the Negroes and the aristocrats. He said: "Ann, you are just about the prettiest colored woman I ever saw. You are too white to be a Negro and married to one." At first, Ann did not speak, but just walked past him as if he wasn't there. He followed us, trying to persuade her to stop and talk to him, and saying he wanted to be a friend to her. I could tell that Ann was very angry.

As we approached the stile that went over the corporation fence, he rushed by us and stood on the steps, blocking our passage. I climbed over the wire fence. Ann handed the laundry over a bundle at a time, and I put it in the tin wagon.

I thought she was going to climb the fence after me. Instead she pulled the hat-pin from her hat. She stood for a moment looking at the man. She screamed at him: "Perry, if you don't get out of my way, I will ram this hat-pin through you." She started towards him. He cleared the stiles. She walked over about ten feet from him. He said: "I just wanted to be a friend to you." He went off in another direction. I hadn't seen Ann so angry before.

She said: "There is nothing as low as poor white trash. That is why they don't allow them to work in the corporation. They are just as the rich people say they are. They don't allow them to even knock at the front door. Whatever they have to sell they have to bring to the back door. I don't blame them." By this time we were in the colored settlement. We had to pass through it. There was a white woman with a mother hubbard style dress on like most of the mountain women wore. She had a coal oil can in one hand and a tin in the other. Ann said: "Ely, you see her?" I said: "Yes." She said: "That is Aunt Liz. She is selling whiskey called moonshine, fifteen cents a drink only to Negroes. She is a kind old woman, but there isn't nothing a sager won't stoop low enough to do."

70

It was almost dark when we got home. Ann started to cook dinner. I had to break up kindling for starting the fire next morning. Someone called from the gate: "Ann." I rushed in the house to the kitchen and told Ann there was someone at the gate calling her. I didn't even look to see who it was.

She went to the door and asked what he wanted. Perry said: "Ann, come here. I just got to talk to you." Ann became furious. She began to swear. I sat on the steps. She went and got the pistol, and came back to the door.

She said: "Perry if you don't leave me alone and leave my gate, I will shoot you." He retorted back: "That's just what you will have to do. No Negro's going to shoot no white man. You better not." At that moment, she shot. I saw the fellow whirl around, almost going to his knees.

I ran up to Ann, saying: "You hit him." I knew she had never shot a gun before. She trembled, holding the gun in her hand. We could hear him running toward the poor white town. Ann said: "I bet he won't trouble another Negro woman."

She said: "This could cause trouble." I said: "Ann, I am going for help." I had heard the Negroes say we don't dare do anything to white people. I thought of what Mr. Rosborough had said: if she ever need him just let him know.

I broke away out of house going to Mr. Rosborough. I had to run a half mile. As I entered the main street, about half way to his house, I heard the sound of a galloping horse. It was Mr. Rosborough going home from the store. I stood out in the road with my hands up. He stop.

I was so excited I couldn't hardly talk at first. When I

was able I told him what happened. He said: "Did she kill him?" I told him: "He ran away." He was a fine strong man. He reached for my hand. With very little effort he swung me up back of him.

He said: "We will have to go a mile around to the gates, I think. I had better go to the village and stop anything that might be brewing. Then we'll get to Ann later." He turned his horse around and headed for the poor white settlement in full gallop.

When we reached the village there was a gathering in front of the big store. Perry was standing in the middle of them with a bandage around his head. We rode up to them. Mr. Rosborough said to Perry: "How bad are you hurt?" He said: "Not too bad. I am lucky. That nigger buck Jake shot me for nothing."

Another man said: "The bullet just grazed him. Left a scalping job. It only stunned him. We are going to teach that nigger a lesson. No nigger is going to shoot a white man in Tennessee and get away with it. You aristocrats pet the nigger. They are so high-collared that they have to be put back in their place. We will hang that nigger to one of those trees. You know we are right, Mr. Rosborough."

Mr. Rosborough sat quietly looking strait at Perry and the fellow that was talking so much. I had never seen him before. There was about twenty men in the gathering. Mr. Rosborough spoke with a voice of authority: "You listen to what I have to say. I know and you know that a Negro don't have any right of law in the South. Only where some white people support him for justice. We people that believe in justice do protect them when they are in the right. Ann was in her own rights when she shot you,

Perry. You have lied about it all. Jake, her husband, has been in Texas three weeks."

Perry said: "It must have been one of her brothers. A nigger buck shot me as I was passing her house." Mr. Rosborough spoke again. "This is a lie. Those two men, her brothers, are on their jobs and won't off until eight-thirty. Now, I am asking you to drop this from your minds. There has never been any trouble between Negroes and white people here. These Negroes that live here love Sewanee and Sewanee people love them. I warn you: if you start any trouble with them you will have to face the military academy bullets and bayonets. I and many of my colleagues will be on guard."

He said to Perry: "You should be ashamed to tell that lie. She chased you today with a hat-pin. You are lucky that she didn't kill you."

He rode away from them in haste to our house. When we arrived the house was dark. He called out and Ann answered. He dismounted and we went in. He told Ann that she would have plenty of protection, that he would be back soon. She should cover all windows with quilts so no one could see anyone from a distance.

He rode away. Soon he returned with eight other horsemen. They called Ann out to talk to her, and told her they would patrol the place that night—which they did. There was never any more about it. That is the real Sewanee as it was controlled back fifty years ago.

Next week was Commencement Week. The entertainments were numerous. The colored people went to see the styles that the ladies from other colleges wore and the different dances. It was something to see.

I went with Ann one night. It was very cold to stand outside and look in the windows. Most people came in carriages. Some came with oil-burning lanterns. That was the only illumination there was in the town.

When it started a gentleman came out where we colored were standing on boxes looking through the windows. He told us to go to the stage entrance and go sit on the stage. I heard one person say: "Thank you, Mr. Hodson." We filed in. It was a beautiful sight. Frenzy Hall could accommodate two hundred couples at one time.

Ann was much amused. She knew every lady in Sewanee. She said: "Don't Miss Carrie and Miss Bessie Kirby Smith look beautiful? And Miss Hodson, Cary Tucker, Dora Colmore, Kary Johnson, McCrady?" She served almost all these ladies in some way.

This was the first time I realized something about me that was not fair—white people just let a Negro go so far and no farther, though we were a part of them and they were a part of us. Why were we at a handicap? No answer. I had worn out the patience out of everybody asking questions.

CHAPTER

6

The next week I left Sewanee for Bridgeport, Alabama, with my dog Tepsy.

All the way on the train I was wondering if I will meet anybody that know me, and know that I am a bastard or will call me a clabber. Would Uncle Tom be like Grandpa? Won't talk and won't allow me to ask questions? He was a business man. I hadn't seen a Negro that was a business man. He must be great. I would learn to ride horses. And I would go to school.

When I come back to Sewanee, I thought, I will be a man, and won't have to take anything off nobody. No one will call me a bastard nor a clabber.

When I arrived, Uncle Tom met me. We walk to his house. Mama hugged me and Tepsy. She was so glad to have us with her. I met the boy, name Readie, that Uncle Tom was raising. I knew he was a bastard, so I knew we had something in common. We could pass for brothers— both had red, curly hair. We were also the same size. He was the oldest. We liked each other and became to be pals. He didn't like to talk and never asked about nothing.

Uncle Tom had a nice house of six rooms. He had four teams of mules for horse-and-buggys, which he often rented to drummers that want to go to Pittsburg, five miles away. The stable was a bit dilapidated. He had three men on his payroll that hauled freight goods to the stores, and also coal.

I was given my first task that afternoon. Readie and I had to arise at four o'clock every morning to feed the stock. I was soon taught how to curry the mules. Uncle Tom taken a liking to me. He said I was quick to move. The colored people were very nice, too. No one ever called me a bastard.

Sunday morning Uncle Tom's sister came by the house going to church. Mama ask her to take me with her. I was made ready. I always went to church on Sunday. I hadn't been to any other than the Episcopal church. This was a Baptist church where Aunt Becky was taking me. I had never seen people shout the "Hala lua" way.

We went in church. We sat very close up front. Soon a long, tall, black man with white hair rose from his chair and gave out some words that they sang. Each word sounded like ten words in one. I couldn't take no part in this singing. When it was finished he read from the Bible a verse, and then his text. He talk for a few minutes, very calm, explaining the scripture.

And then, all at once, he let out a yell, saying: "Whoever believeth in me shall have everlasting life." At this, all over the church people were crying out: "Amen." "Thank God." I looked about, wondering what it was all about.

Soon, the Parson was moaning and groaning his words out. He would stomp his foot and come forward with

76

another yell. By this time the hand-clapping and Amens were so loud you couldn't hear what the Parson was really saying.

He put his hand to the side, and yelled out: "Who is going to be ready when Gabriel blows the trumpet?" Aunt Becky slammed her pocketbook and hat into my lap, and leapt to her feet with a scream, dashing by me into the aisle. Two more sisters done the same thing.

I ran out of the church, and went down the road, running. When I looked back I saw three boys back of me. I waited for them to catch up. They ask me: what was I running away for? I told them I thought my Auntie had gone crazy. I wanted to get away. They told me that these people was happy and was shouting for joy.

So, I went back. I would not go in the church. I waited outside for Aunt Becky to come out. When she did she was acting like she did before she went in. On the way home Aunt Becky told me that this was Negro religion—the only religion where you felt the Holy Spirit moving in your body.

She explained to me that when the Holy Spirit touches you, you can't be still. You just have to let everybody know it. She also said Episcopalians were not Christians. No white people were Christians. They don't know what the Holy Ghost is. I would have to experience it for myself.

When I got home I went to Mama Mat. I wanted to know if the white people at Sewanee was all lying about them being God's children. Aunt Becky said no white people were Christians. Everybody laughed at me today for running out of church. I didn't know that Negroes were the only people that had the Holy Ghost. I sure want this religion.

Here I started to asking Uncle Tom about religion. He soon got tired of trying to answer. He said: "White people teach Negroes what they want them to know. That will help them to be more of service to the white people. That's why most Negroes is willing for the whites to have all this world. Just give the Negroes heaven. A good nigger should go to heaven."

I was determined that if I had to be a Negro I would be as much like them as I could be. I would go to church and Sunday School. I would be touched by the Holy Ghost and shout like the others.

During the next week I began to see more of the colored people. Many men that was out of work hung around the livery stable, hoping there would be a chance to do some work for Uncle Tom. This was the first time I had seen a crap game. They would play cards and shoot craps when Uncle Tom was out. I wouldn't tell about it. Every body seemed to like me. I was quite happy.

I did not have any time to play with children or go to school. Uncle started a junk yard. He taught me to weigh material. This I ran almost alone for about six months. He often sent me with the horse-and-buggy to Pittsburg when a drummer rented it.

One thing I missed that was so different in the people there and the people at Sewanee: no one wore a collar and tie. Most colored wore blue overalls. The only ones that wore suits were the preacher, the school teacher and the barber for white people.

78

In Sewanee everybody except Grandpa and Bill Smith was always dressed. I had never seen any white man that lived in the Corporation on the street without a collar and tie, and no students either.

I hadn't seen a white man drunk until I came to Bridgeport. There were no coachmen and no colored men driving carriages with their madams sitting by them in Bridgeport. There wasn't ladies, carrying parasols with ruffles, nor ladies dressed in white suits with shirt waists and fluted collars and cuffs.

In Sewanee I use to love to look at these ladies when they taken their evening walk. I always liked to hear them say: "Hello, Ely," when I tipped my cap. This I missed very much in Bridgeport. White people there taken no part of the colored people. No colored people ever said anything good about the whites. They talked as if they hated white people.

I was having a struggle within: trying to get this Negro religion worked out, and learning to hate white people, after I had been taught that they were all God's children and we are to love everybody.

I didn't have any bitter feeling toward anyone in Bridgeport. I was never called a bastard by anyone. I pray to become a Christian like the Negro. For months I went to prayer meeting at church.

I heard the confessing of converts, telling of their experience of being borned again: how a little white man, who looked like Christ, placed a small stone on their tongue and the salvation went over them and God told them that they had been borned again. Then they would shout until they sometimes would pass out unconscious.

79

I prayed and prayed that I would become to be like they were. I became to be so nervous that I would have dreams that the world was coming to an end. I would awake screaming, leaping out of the bed. I would wake Mama Mat, asking: did she hear Gabriel blowing his trumpet? "What can I do. I am a sinner."

Mama sent me to talk to Reverend Walker, who was called Parson. She said: "You don't have Father Eastern to guide you, so go to the Parson." I did.

He listened to me, then said: "Son, just keep praying the Holy Ghost is working on you. It works in mysterious ways. So keep praying." I did just that. This lasted over a year.

I had not gone to school, as was promised. This was the winter of 1906. Readie and I worked hard. When coal was sold at apartment houses, we had to carry it in scuttles up two and three stories. It taken all day to carry a ton up and dump it in the bins. This we had to do frequently.

I had still in my mind to go to Dr. Towson's school at Winchester. I started begging Mama Mat and Uncle Tom to let me go there and live with Aunt Adline.

There were two brothers by the name Pain. I liked them very much. Jonny Pain got married to a lady name Annie Sick. All the men kidded him, saying: "Pain is Sick." He did not like this kidding. In a small cemetary in Bridgeport to this day are two small tombstones, side by side. The inscribing reads: "Pain and Sick" by Ripley, believe it, or not.

That spring Uncle Tom leased four hundred acres for farm land. He hired men to cultivate it. He gave me ten acres and Readie the same. We could have the money that it brought.

This increased our task. We had to be up by three-thirty every morning to feed ten head of mules, so they could leave by six o'clock for the fields two miles away. The men had a contract at one dollar a day to work ten hours in the field. They also got one meal a day which was at mid-day. I had to take it to them.

I work my crop in the afternoon, and had good luck. I raised pumpkins and corn which I sold for a total of twenty dollars. This would help me to go to school in Winchester. The harvesting was over in October, and I began carrying coal and helping with the freight hauling.

Anderson was one of the teamsters for Uncle Tom. One day he was unloading a barrel of sorgum molasses. It got out of control, rolled against the curb, and bursted. The storekeeper it was intended for become angry, and started kicking Anderson. Anderson picked up the end-gate, and struck the white man across the head. The man fell on the sidewalk.

Many white men came running to where this had happened. Anderson ran toward the colored part of town. The white was yelling: "Kill that nigger." I was holding the team as usual. I drove the team to the stable.

Anderson had gone home, got his gun, and had told other people what happened. Then, he left town.

Soon, ten white men and two blood hounds came up to the stable. They were going after Anderson. This was the first time I had seen colored people so angry with white people. They cursed and swore at each other. Almost every colored person had a gun. They did not catch Anderson.

Later the law came back without Anderson, and there was a rejoycing among the colored men. They sat around talking of how they hated white people. I listened, thinking.

One fellow said: "I keep my gun always handy. If I ever have trouble with them, they may kill me but I bet I'll take some with me when I go."

I thought this was just about the most sensible thing I had heard any of them say. This would be what I would do when I grew up: buy a good gun and learn to use it.

I began to think: "These Negroes are right. White people are all evil and wrong—they are not Christians at all. I must become to be converted in this Negro religion. I must. I hate white people. They are the cause of me being a bastard. If I ever get back to Father Eastern, I will tell him how wrong his teaching is. White people don't know anything about the Holy Ghost." I thought about my mother being converted when she was near death—how the Spirit had moved her, caused her to be able to shout and clap her hands. I prayed and prayed that this miracle would happen to me.

I knew that in Winchester colored people were like those in Bridgeport. I would soon be like them, although some people knew I am a bastard. That wouldn't mean anything when I was like other Negroes—Christian like them and could shout. This I kept in mind.

Two weeks later I was told that I could go to Winchester. Thanksgiving had just passed. Uncle Tom gave me an Ingersol watch and chain and a suit of clothes. This was the first time I had worn a new suit of clothes. I had to leave my dog which I regreted much. I went all alone.

I got to Winchester at two o'clock the same afternoon. Aunt Adline met me at the train. She was a little hunchbacked lady. She spoke very few words at any time, and was a devout Baptist.

She showed me where I was to sleep. Then, she taken her scissors and ript open my pocket that Mama had sewed my money up in. There was eighteen dollars.

I liked her house—only three rooms. She owned an organ. As we were about to have dinner we heard shouts out in the street. We went out to see what it was.

There was a young girl about sixteen screaming and shouting, yelling: "I have been borned again." There was about fifteen older people following her home. Aunt Adline ran out and hugged her, saying: "God bless you." I stood and looked on with envy: "Oh, if I could only be like her to have people loving me like that, and knowing that I am a child of God. And knowing that I could prove it."

We went in the house to eat. I was very silent. Aunt Adline said: "That preacher and his wife has converted a lot of people during this betracted meeting. It will be over tonight." I said: "I sure wish I could go. I want to be converted." She said: "You were born an Episcopalian. You don't know what you are talking about. If you want to go church tonight, you can go with Virginia. You know her from Sewanee where she worked at the Tucker boarding house. She will be over here soon, and will take you. You can learn about Methodist religion."

Virginia came and took me to her house. She seem to

look at me as if she was trying to keep from laughing about something. Although she was pleasant, she kidded me a bit about wanting to be converted.

When we went in the church the only seats unoccupied were in the back. We were seated. I had never seen a Methodist meeting in operation. The lady preacher opened the service, giving the text: "The Eagle teareth up his nest." This lady and her husband was known as the sin-killing pair, travelling through the South, saving souls. They were from Atlanta, Georgia. They explained the superiority of eagles, comparing their traits of training their young with the way God teaches his own to bring them into his fold.

When the sermon was over, Reverend Washington ask all sinners to stand up. Virginia told me: "Stand up." I did. Then he ask everyone that wanted to be prayed for to come forward, beckoning with his hand. Virginia told me to go to him. This was strange to me. I wasn't sure of what I was doing.

I went up just in front of a colored woman named Mat Lu Gray that I knew from Sewanee. She was a good dancer. She and Ann had been friends. I felt much better now.

When we reached the preacher there were many people on their knees praying that hadn't been converted from nights before. They sat on another bench. We were told to sit. I sat by Mat Lu. We were told: "Kneel and pray." Here was when I was confused. I only knew the Lord's prayer. I began to listen to what Mattie Lu was saying, and I would say: "Me too, Lord."

Soon there were many people around us singing songs

84

I had never heard, and clapping their hands. This went on for hours. Mattie Lu prayed. I kept saying: "Me too, Lord." Sometimes I couldn't hear what she was saying, but I would say "Me too" anyway. All at once Mattie Lu jumped up and started shouting. I jumped up and began jumping and watching her, trying to do everything she was doing, although I didn't scream. Soon they pulled her down. I was still jumping when they led me to a bench, and I sat down.

I looked around for Virginia. She was lying on a bench cracking her sides with laughter. The preacher came to me, asking me: "Are you the boy that came through tonight?" I ask: "Through what?" He said: "How do you feel?" I said: "Alright, only it is too hot in here." The preacher turned away and said no more.

Soon we started for home. It was bitter cold outside and had snowed. Virginia taken me home with her for the night, and next morning took me to Aunt Adline to tell her I had confessed religion. She was still laughing. Aunt Adline said: "This boy don't know anything about no religion." My confession was over.

That morning many people came to congratulate me. Auntie would tell them I didn't know what I was doing. This caused a lot of argument. Some said Aunt Adline didn't want to admit my confession because I was converted in a Methodist church. This all became disgusting and shameful.

Next morning I ask Aunt Adline to let me to go to Sewanee. "I have made you so unhappy with your friends. I want to go and talk to Father Eastern. I will come back later." First she refused, telling me she had a job for me where I would be given my meals and fifty cents a week and could go to school. She would get two dollars and a half a week cooking at the Nortons' boarding house.

I pleaded: "Let me go. I just have to go. Nobody understands like Father Eastern and Father Gerry." We were standing by the window looking at the snow-covered field. I said: "I hate white people like all Negroes. But I need to talk to Father." She look at me for a moment, then she said: "Perhaps it will be best for you. Don't ever say you hate white people. They are not all bad. My best friends are white people. All colored people have some white friends that are good."

Next morning I left Winchester at eleven o'clock and arrived in Sewanee at five o'clock that afternoon. I went to my stepfather's house. He was home. My little brothers had grown a lot since I was gone. They were all glad to see me. My stepfather wanted to know what happened to me that I came alone. I told him I came to see Father Eastern.

It was almost dark by this time. I told him I was going to Father Eastern's house, and would be back soon. When I knocked on Father's door he opened it. He seemed so glad to see me. He spoke kindly, saying: "How have you been? Why didn't you write me. You have grown a lot. It's been over two years since you left here."

There was something of interest in his talk, and I realized that I hadn't felt it since I had seen him last. He said: "Did you go to school?" I told him: "No." He said: "Why not?" I said: "Father, I had to come because I have to tell you white people are wrong, and you have taught me wrong about religion."

Father was sipping a cup of tea. He set the cup down,

86

missing the saucer. Looking straight at me, he said: "What are you trying to say, Ely?"

I stood to my feet: "Father, you people have these schools in big buildings here in Sewanee. You say you are teaching Christianity, but you don't know what the Holy Ghost is. You people are not Christian. You don't know nothing about religion like the Negroes. They have a religion that the Holy Ghost makes them shout until they pass out. They talk with God. He touches with Salvation and the Holy Ghost. I have heard them say that God has told them they have been borned again. I have been so disappointed because I could not get this religion. Many has said I was too much like you white people. They say the world is coming to an end, and I am a sinner. All Negroes hate white people. I am the same way. I just wanted to come and tell you I made a fool of myself at Winchester trying to be like them and this Negro religion. I was to go to school there, but after making such a fool of myself I had to come and talk with you."

Father finished sipping his tea. He was smiling. He rose from the desk, and sat in his big chair by the fire. He said: "Ely, I am glad you came to me at this time. You are turning fifteen years old. I realize you understand much better now about many things. Now I can talk to you with much more ease than before. First, I will explain to you about Negro religion, which you will never be able to understand. You have everything all wrong as I will prove to you. We will talk about you. This is why it is hard for you to understand the Negroes—you are somewhat like a man building a building who trys to start at the top instead of the bottom. That is the way you have started out. You would not go to school which is the basic training. You have been about a cultured class of people, and for that reason you have skipped the primary part of your training."

I listened hard to Father.

He went on: "So, now I can explain to you better than I could before. The Negroes are still very much instinctive. It is native nature for them to sing tunes and be demonstrative and emotional. Like almost all natives they have some trait of songs that has a stimulating or hypnotic effect causing them to exert themselves into exortions. Take the Indian, for instance. They would sing and dance all night to drown out the fear of dying the next day in battle. I don't condemn any religion, but I don't agree that all religions are really of true Christianity. The Negro learned his teaching of God from the white people. They have annexed to it much of their native habit of hypnotics. That was helpful during slavery because they could magnify their thoughts until they believed almost anything that they wished would come to be. That was wonderful. It gave them hope."

He paused.

Then, he went on: "Those dreams you had were caused by your anxiety and your believing that you would be like them. Ely, this was what is called taxation of the mind. I haven't ever heard of any man or woman that has seen God or even talked to him since Christ. No one knows there is a God. We can only believe. Negroes do not hate white people. Some may say they do, but it can't be true. How could they live without their white friends? So don't ever say you hate anybody. I want you to join the choir at

88

our church. Forget all about the experience you had. There are many religions and teachings of religions. Most people are demonstrative as to their intelligence. Understand that all of us are God's children. Our task is to love everybody. This is all God's world."

Just then, the clock of Breslin Tower was striking nine o'clock. Father said: "Come see me often." He walked to the door with me.

I started to walk back to my stepfather's house. It was cold. I didn't feel as I did before I went to see Father Eastern. I only felt sorry for anybody that was a Negro. My mind went back to the day I was first called a nigger. I decided I would never be a Negro—I would not be somebody people were sorry for. I would be a man in the eyes of man and God. From that very night I refused to answer to the word Negro.

CHAPTER
7

I was glad to be back in Sewanee.

I didn't even think of being a bastard which I knew I would be called. I decided: "I am a big boy now. I don't have to take anything I don't want to. I can fight my way if I have to."

My stepfather was still up waiting for me. He talked about Alabama and about me going to see Father Eastern. He hadn't been out of Sewanee in twenty years. He was an Episcopalian and didn't know anything about other denominations. I tried to tell him about how people acted in Alabama. He was like Grandpa in some ways. He was eliterate. He could not write his own name.

He told me Grandpa had married since I left—a young girl seventeen years old and they had a baby girl. He said: "Ned will kill hogs tomorrow. We will go and help him. He will kill over twenty. The old man is doing good, tough as times are. This panic makes things mighty tough." I hadn't heard much about there being a panic.

I went to see Grandpa the next morning. He was glad to see me. He and his wife ask me wouldn't I like to live with them? I told them yes, until Mama Mat came back to Sewanee.

Grandpa said my job for the day was to keep the kettles boiling so there would be lots of hot water to scald the hogs. Men were making ready to start killing. I loved to be around a hog-killing. I like to broil the melts over the blaze and eat them.

Many people came. Grandpa always had the biggest killing of anybody in the town. Everyone that came he gave parcels of meat to take home.

When the work was over Grandpa paid everybody in cash. This no one expected because script was being used. He was praised highly for this. I thought about what he had told me—when you got money you are somebody. He was somebody that day even if he was a Negro.

He brought out a gallon of whiskey. The men drank. They helped him load twelve hogs on the wagon. He taken to market. That was all he could sell. The butcher didn't need any more. He was unhappy with himself, for not killing before Thanksgiving. He said: "Most everybody is leaving here next week. School is out."

He had to accept a due bill of script instead of money. This caused him to boast, which I liked to hear him say: "Old Ned has got his own money. No banker can't tell me when I can have my money. You just be like me, boy."

He had ten hogs to cure. I had to keep the fire burning for rendering lard and condement dip for curing smoke meat. We had to grind sausage. This lasted for three weeks. The smell of grease became almost sickening. We saved all the meat so it could be sold by pieces.

Every day Grandpa was teaching me to milk. He had twelve milk cows. I had to milk the three with small tits. He was kinder to me than he had been.

Finally, all the meat was either in the salt bins or in the smoke house. The next day we sawed wood and piled it outside the house—enough for three or four days supply. He checked the food for the stock. He rode away next morning not telling anyone where he was going. When he came back he had two jugs of whiskey that he put in the feed bin at the barn. That evening, when he went to deliver milk, Ever, his wife, told me she thought he was going on a drunk. We would have to look after things for him.

Everything was so much different than before. The house was clean. He didn't sit on the floor to eat off the hearth like he did before he married. But he still ate his possums. The bed tickings wasn't leaves or straw like they used to be—we had feather ticks to sleep on. I was enjoying living with them. Ever was a good housekeeper.

That night at dinner Ever began begging him not to drink too much. He boasted how he could take care of himself and all of us. I had to laugh when he said he was a money man.

He wanted all his children from there on named after money. "Money is power." His daughter by his second wife was named Goldie. "This daughter we have Ever, is named Silverine. The next one you have we will name her Greenback. That's our job—getting green back." We all gigled. Soon we went to bed.

Next morning it was bitter cold. When we finished milking, Grandpa told me he wanted me to go with him to Mrs. Emma Tucker's house which he looked after when they went away for the winter. I did not have any overcoat. Ever gave me a blanket to wrap up in. On the way he told me that we must examine every window. We had to examine every water pitcher and slop jar to see that there was no water left in them.

The people had left a week ago. He had been so busy curing meat that he hadn't had time to look after the house. He said: "There is around eighteen rooms. You can go up and down the steps faster than I. I hope that it hasn't been cold enough to freeze water inside until now." We found many containers with water in them just like the students had left them. Nothing had frozen. We covered some furniture and left.

We went to see Ada, his oldest daughter, that had been living in Tulahoma and had moved to Sewanee while I was in Alabama. Mother Richerson had hired her to work like my mother had worked. She had a daughter one month older than I. I hadn't seen much of them after my mother died. Aunt Ada was very fond of me. I did not realize it until that day when she said: "You must come with me to see Mother Richerson. She asks about you often. She is getting very old and feeble, and she can't hardly walk."

We went in to Mother Richerson's living room. There she sat tatting threads just like I had always seen her when I was a small boy. Polly, her parrot, began saying: "Polly wants a cracker." Aunt said: "Mother, I have someone that come to see you."

I had walked beside her, saying: "How are you, Mother?" Her eyes were not too good. She look around, and said: "Why haven't you been to see me before now? Remember that I am your Godmother. It's been four years since you have been to see me. You have grown much. You are a fine looking boy. Mat is doing a fine job raising

93

you. She is a fine woman. I have heard that you don't like school. You could read when you were five, and write. Remember the slate you got for Christmas? Every thing you wrote for awhile was all capital letters. Your mother Lena said about your first writing that it looked a sign painter's work. Too bad you don't like school."

Just then Dr. Richerson came crippling in assisted by his cane. He used some profanity almost every word he spoke. As he hobbled in the doorway he said: "What the hell is all the talk about?" Mother Richerson answered: "Your little boy has come to see us."

He had come closer to where we were. He was very near-sighted. He looked, and say: "Who are you?" Then he said: "You damn little scamper. Have you forgot how you used to come to the back door of the store and beg for lemon drops and marshmallows?" On the table by which he was standing there was a box of candy. He tossed a bar of chocolate at me, which I caught.

He ask me: "How did you like Alabama?" I told him I did not like any part of it because the people were not like Sewanee. "They don't dress like Sewanee people. They don't wear collars and ties. They don't have servants like you people here." Dr. Richerson gave a grunt: "What do that class of sagers know about servants? They are too listless to get out of the rain. That's why we don't have anything to do here with them, damn them."

Mother said: "Ely, have you been to see Father Gerry?" I said: "No, I have seen Father Eastern." She said: "We are going to loose Father Gerry soon. He is going to South Carolina to become to be Bishop. We are so sorry that we have to loose him. He has presided at St. Augustus so long."

94

Then she said: "Ely, you must go to school. When Bishop Gailor comes here Easter, I am going to see if he can't have you go to St. Mary's school at Nashville. You can help work your way through. I have heard that you are smart, and like to work. Lena, your mother, was all set on you being educated. She was an unusual colored girl. She was like my own. She started you so young to learn to read and write. You were her pride and joy. I want to help you and there are other people that will help you."

She said to my Aunt Ada: "There is a bundle of clothes in the cellar for Ely that Mrs. Susie Huntington sent for him—some of Ellery, her oldest boy's clothes. Give them to him." She sat there by the window as she had for many years, and my thoughts went back to when my mother and she was so close.

The sleet was blowing against the panes. It was so cold outside. This warmness of real friendship within could never be forgotten by a small black boy. I knelt and kissed her hand as it rested on the arm of her wheelchair. She turned her face to the window, as I said good-bye.

When we got to the servant quarters Auntie's husband and Grandpa was much pepped up from their drinks. Grandpa was full of boast. He was very proud that he had a wife thirteen years younger than his oldest daughter. I unrolled my bundle. There was many things I needed, above all an overcoat which I had never owned. This was a day I could never forget.

We left for home. The wind was high, but the sleet had stopped. Grandpa didn't pay any attention to the cold. I got very cold before we got home. Grandpa only mumbled to himself now and then. I thought he would fall off the wagon. He would lean over very far, then straiten up again. When we got home he drove the horse under the shed. He didn't unhitch him as it wouldn't be long before he would have to take milk to four people.

When we went in the house Ever had dinner ready. What a dinner: backbones, cabbage, cracked cornbread, peach cobler, butter milk!

While we were eating the wind had eased. It had started to snow. By the time we had finished milking the ground was covered white. After measuring the milk Grandpa decided he would use the sulky to deliver the milk. It would be lighter for the horse to pull in the snow. He drove away, taking a jug of whiskey with him.

Ever did not have anything to say to me for a while. I got busy carving a figure-four tripper for a bird trap. About two hours passed. Ever stood looking out at the snow.

She said: "That old girl is sure picking geese this evening. What a snow!" Then, she said: "Ely, I think your Grandfather is going on a drunk. If he does you and I will have to look after things for him. He does that about every three months. It will last about two days, then he will be alright for another three months."

She walked to the window, looked out, and said: "He is back. I see the horse at the gate." We waited for a half hour. No one came in. She said: "Go to the barn and see what's keeping him." I went. He was not there. I went back and I ask: "Do you think he might have fallen off the sulky?" She said: "Take the horse and lead him on the trail through the woods. If he fell off he will be lying in the road. I would go with you but I can't leave the baby for long."

I started through the woods. The snow was almost blinding. The trees on each side of the trail guided the horse. Just as we reached the brook I stopped. I tried to get the sulky across the stream, but the horse would not move toward the stream. He just balked. I started to walk to the stream and stumbled over Grandpa, covered in the snow.

I rolled him over, and brushed the snow off of him. He was breathing, although he was out of understanding, and didn't say a word. He was limp as a rag. I couldn't lift him into the sulky. He would freeze if he was left for long.

I thought about in Bridgeport how Uncle Tom hauled all dead stock to the bone-yard when snow was on the ground. I would drag Grandpa—anything would drag easy in snow that deep. I turned the horse around and backed the sulky over Grandpa. I taken the reins off the horse and tied Grandpa to the axle of the sulky. It was hard to raise him enough to get the reins under him, around his body and under his shoulder. I finally got him to a sitting position and tied him. Then I led the horse up the trail home.

Ever and I drug him into the house. She made a pile of thick comforters in front of the fireplace, and let him lie there until he sobered up. Ever was angry. She didn't talk at all. I made two figure-four trap trippers to catch snow-birds with.

At one o'clock Grandpa got up and drank two dippers of water. No one spoke. I went to the kitchen, and went to bed.

Next morning Grandpa called to me to go and milk. This was something I was getting tired of. My hands got so cold. At breakfast Ever told him how I went and got him out of the snow. She said he should be ashamed to have his grandson bring him home drunk. She threatened to leave him if he ever done this again. I left them quarreling, and went to set some traps for birds.

When I came back, as I came in the door, I heard him say: "Yes, I will buy you that churn, the one you can rock with your foot. Is there anything else you need from town." Ever said: "No, but I want seventy five cents tomorrow. That lady that comes from Tulahoma that straitens hair will be here in Sewanee. I want to have my hair straitened. I want a dollar to buy a spare comb and twenty-five cents for a box of grease. Ely can stay with the baby while I am gone."

Grandpa said his pet word: "God-ding woman, are you trying to break me? When you lived in Beans Creek you didn't know what hair straitening, combs and grease was." Ever threw the dish at him that she was holding in her hand.

Out he went calling me to come on. As I caught up with him he mumbled: "I believe in the Communion of Saints but not the Resurrection." We hitched up the team and started to town. I had to ask him why didn't he believe in the Resurrection? "That is when I am going to see my mother again."

He said: "Boy, I want you to be a man like me. You talk like these white people here in Sewanee. That's what's wrong with Ever. Everybody that comes to Sewanee gets all high-collared. She wants to spend two dollars for her hair. She is as pretty as a peach like she is."

He gave me my first lesson about women: "I will have

98

to give it to her, because the thing about women is—you can't hardly live with them and, god-ding, you can't live without them. That's why the scripture say, 'a man born of a woman is only in this world a few days, and his heart is filled with trouble.' That is true. And I mean trouble. When you are grown don't let no woman boss you. Be like me."

We stopped in front of the Fecher Hardware store. He went in. I stayed on the wagon to hold the horses. He stayed so long I got cold. I hitched the team to the post and went in. He and Mr. Fecher were at the back of the store where the stove was.

Grandpa was boasting as usual. He was telling about me. What a fine son he had. How I had found him in the snow when he was hurt falling from the sulky, and how I brought him home. He was going to take me from Mattie Davis. I was his flesh-and-blood. He would fight a lawsuit up to five hundred dollars to get me.

I had come in quietly, and neither one heard me. I stood back and listened. When he finished, he ask Mr. Fecher wasn't he right to take me. "He figures my books. He told me how much I owed you to a tee."

Mr. Fecher said: "Ned, I can't say that you are exactly right. Everybody knows Mat taken him when he was a small boy when no one wanted him. Now he is large enough to be of help. He's about fifteen years old. She done fine with him. He was in here about a month ago when he come back. He deposit fifty cents on a air gun, and said he would pay along as he made money. He could have taken the gun if he had ask because several of corporation white people has told me to let him have anything he

99

wanted that a boy should have. He is a courteous little fellow, and a fine looking chap. I think you will have trouble trying to take him from her."

They came to the front of the store. I was leaning on the counter looking up at the air guns in the rack behind the counter. Mr. Fecher said: "Hello." I bowed to him. Grandpa picked up part of the churn and told me to bring the rack it set in and the rocker.

We had got on the wagon when Mr. Fecher came out of the store with an air gun in his hand. He said: "Wait, Ned." He handed me the gun and a bag with shots in it, saying: "You owe me a dollar and a half. You can pay when you get it." I could have shouted. I wanted this gun so bad. I thanked him. He looked as if he really enjoyed letting me have this gun.

Grandpa drove all the way home, not saying anything to me direct. He mumbled once or twice, and I knew he was not happy. I was so happy to think that somebody thought something of me. Grandpa had told Mr. Fecher that I had saved his life. For the first time I had come to really love him.

He hadn't all day told me to shut up. And I had a gun. My hands were cold holding the gun, but I just couldn't lay it down. Just to think it was mine. When Tepsy came from Alabama we would hunt. I would have no babies to care for. I was a big boy now.

Ever was happy to get her rocker churn. When she saw my gun, she said: "Did Ned buy it for you?" I told her I got it on credit. "Why didn't you pay for it? You had fourteen dollars when you came to Sewanee. What did you do with it?" I told her that money was to go to school on.

"I gave it to Father to keep until Mama Mat comes. I cannot use it." I helped her wash and set up the churn.

Grandpa was busy out in the smoke house. When he came in Ever was sitting holding Silverine, the baby, in her lap and rocking the churn with her foot. He had a basket full of dried berries and roots which he said were herbs. He stood looking at Ever operating the churn with her foot.

She said: "Mr. Berry was here and said if you wanted to ship some butter to Nashville you could. The creamery will pay fifteen cents a pound, but won't pay the express on less than twenty pounds." She went on: "You see, we have so much milk on hand. It's a shame to have to feed it to the hogs and chickens. We have fourteen gallons every day, and for the next three months you will only sell three gallon a day. I can make butter out of all of it much easier with this churn."

Grandpa said: "God-ding, if you ain't the smartest gal in Sewanee. I am going to give you money for that hair grease." He went to the trunk in the corner of the room, reached in and got a hand full of silver money. He came to the back of her chair placing one hand on her shoulder, bent down and kissed her on the neck. He nudged the baby in the stomach lightly. He was smiling, looking at them. I hadn't ever seen him in this humor before.

He gave her two dollars for her hair. Then, he said: "You can have all the money that you get off the butter. When those Jew pack-peddlers come by you can buy that silk dress that cost ten dollars. I want you to have what you want. Only I don't want you to get so high up on the hog that some of the high-collared niggers will take you away from me."

She look up into his face, and say: "Ned, you are all I want." He ruffled his hand in her hair, picked up his basket and went to the kitchen.

Eight months later she left him. I often wondered if he knew it would happen. I thought it many times.

When Grandpa left the room I went out to see if there were any birds in the traps I set that morning. I found all four traps down. One box had two birds, the others had one each. There was an old parrot cage Grandpa had brought home out of rubbish he had hauled. I taken the birds out alive and put them in it.

I went in the house to show them to Ever, wanting to know if there was enough to make a pie.

Grandpa said: "Don't cook them. I want them to bait traps with. A coon will go through hell to get a bird, and a possum or a fox will too. I am going to teach you how to trap. I have to go into the mountains soon as the snow melts to get herbs. I have to make up some herbs for many people. The herbs I have are too dry. I will go to my herb beds and dig fresh ones. I want to teach you about herbs. Old Ned has to do a lot of things to help people."

Ever said: "Ned, that girl was here to see you while you were gone, poor thing. She said please do something for her." He stood gazing in the fire for a minute, then said: "God-ding these fool gals that let those high-collared niggers mess them up. Then, they come to me asking me to keep them from having a baby. I have helped some. I am good with herbs. But I don't like that kind of business. I'll try to help her, because I do hate to see bastards born."

While he was silent, I was thinking nearly all of my

102

family was bastards. Maybe that was why Grandpa didn't like to be around us any more than he was.

He taken my birds and went to the smoke house. Ever said: "He is a good man and smart, only if he didn't drink. If he would just try to be happy. You have been lots of help since you come. You are going to stay with Mat, aren't you?" I told her: "I belong to Mama Mat. She needs me. She is suffering badly with rhumatism."

Ever said: "Lee, your stepfather, has a letter for you. They read it. Mat will be here the first week in February. I don't want Ned to know it yet. He is so set on taking you from her. I don't think it is right. You are the finest boy I ever knew. You are so much company. But she needs you more than Ned does."

Grandpa came in with four steel traps—two large ones, two small ones. He explained to me that coons and foxes was hard to catch. With a live bird it is a cinch you will catch them. Possum can be caught with anything.

He said: "If it's not too cold tonight we will go possum hunting. We will give Heck and Dan a workout." They were his two dogs.

I went with him to deliver milk. He hum a tune almost all the time. On the way back the old lamp-lighter was lighting the oil lamps at every corner. Grandpa called to him, and stopped the wagon. The old white fellow came to the wagon.

He said: "Ned, everybody leaves Sewanee. Seems but you and me stay to keep it together. You have the night and I have mine at sunrise." I hadn't seen him for five years. I used to follow him around on summer evenings, watching

103

him fill the lamps. He spoke to me: "You are some boy now. You used to keep me company when you was small. I will be seeing you."

We drove on. Grandpa said: "He's got some job keeping lights burning. No Negro could have a job that easy. He is a good man. When he dies they will give him a big military funeral. When I die that will just be the end of a good nigger. White people has the God-dingest ways." I said nothing because I had many things I want to ask Grandpa when we go herb hunting.

After supper we left for Dessom hollow a mile from home. The dogs treed two possums on the way to the hollow. Grandpa carried a ax and I had my air gun. Good thing we did. Just as we entered the hollow the dogs picked up a trail. Five hundred yards ahead they treed a coon up a big black gum tree. We could not climb it.

Grandpa found a rotten log and some spunk that was dry and would burn. We built a fire so bright we could see the coon stretched on a limb. He told me to try to hit it with the air gun. I shot four times before I hit. This frightened the coon, and it ran out to the end of the limb and leapt off, landing in the water. The dogs went in after it.

We rushed to the bank with our lantern and could see the coon trying to drown the dogs. The water was about three feet deep and fifteen feet across. Grandpa pulled off his overcoat, jumped in the water, grabbed the coon by the tail, and started swinging it around over his head until he got to the edge of the water, where he slammed the coon to the ground. The dogs got it. They had a tough fight killing the coon. It was big, weighing twenty two pounds. Grandpa said: "That is the largest coon I ever killed." This was a valuable experience for me because I had to do the same thing several times in the next four years when I was trapping and hunting for a living.

As we walked back home he talked much, telling me that a man has to learn to protect everything he owns.

I ask if he wasn't afraid the coon would bite him. He said: "No, a man that thinks knows he must move faster and can move faster than any animal. He can always beat anything when he is not afraid of it. I am not afraid of anything. I want you to be the same way. Being brave is a man's job. Remember that."

When we got home we put the possum in a barrel. Grandpa skinned it that night. He gave me the skin. I tanned it and had a cap made out of it. I wore it for four years.

Two day later we went to dig herbs. We taken the birds in the cage, the traps and a grubbing hoe. We went below Morgan Steep down the first bank of the mountain where the soil was rich.

Grandpa told me that General Morgan had jumped off that rock. His horse was killed but the general got away. He said: "The Yankees almost caught him. He and his bushwhackers gave them Yankees hell around these canyons. That rock is named after him. Any man that can do that God-ding jump ain't afraid of nothing. It takes brave men to live and do the right thing at the right time."

He said: "This is a good time to dig herbs. I have been getting my herbs here for thirty years. I always take some and leave some to grow more. This you must learn—not to destroy the growth of anything. You can make a living in the mountains if you learn the value of its gifts."

I was so glad to hear him say that because I had this thought in my mind: I had always felt free in the mountains and there was something friendly about them.

He raked the leaves back with a few strokes of the hoe. There were some white roots. He smiled, and said: "These are fine." Breaking a piece off one root he gave it to me, and said: "Chew it." I chewed a piece. It was so bitter, I spit it out. He laughed: "You can learn what all the herbs taste like, and then you will know them. That is quiene root. Over there you see caltrop, catnip, hoorhound, and sasfras.

We collected berries from the catnip and hoorhound, putting each in its own flour sack. He said: "Over there under the grapevines is a myrtle herb. The Indians believed in it. White people call it gensand. It is a medicine good for anything you suffer with. It sells for seven dollars a pound. These mountains is full of this kind of stuff. Everybody around here is too lazy to get it."

We went under the grapevines. There were a lot of dried stalks shaped like the letter Y. He said: "This stalk is gensand. When it is green it has a red flower that is forked. It don't grow in the sunshine. It has to grow in the shade of something."

He dug up a stalk, taking the larger root, placing the smaller one back in the ground. The roots were shaped like human limbs. He stood holding a root that looked like a leg. He said: "That is good for any leg ailment." We had collected seven different herbs. He gave me the hoe, carried the herbs himself.

I had wondered why he brought a jug with him. We walked around to a rocky cliff. There was a tiny stream about an inch wide with a yellow streak in the bottom of it. He dug a hole large enough to sink the jug in. "We will have to wait a while for the jug to fill. This is clevic water. It's called mineral water. It sells for fifty cents a gallon in the summer at the hotels. I use it in my herb teas."

While the jug was filling we walked around to the waterfall. I didn't know it was there. He was looking for something in the stream. Looking in the hole of water I knew that nothing could keep me away from this place that summer. I was happy to think I could make a living in the mountains all on my own. Grandpa had taught me something I would surely do.

He called me to come to him down the stream where there was a bar of sand. He was stooped down, looking. "What kind of track is that there?" I looked, and said: "How could a baby that small come down here?" He laughed: "That's the track of a big coon. It do look like a baby's foot."

We went back to the jug which was full. He said: "This water don't drop like other water—it drops like oil." We went back to the wagon on top. He stood for a minute looking down the canyon, then we drove back toward the corporation.

He said: "We have to go to the other side of the mountain to Shakerag hollow. There will be more coons and possums than you can shake a stick at."

On the way he told me the mountains were full of berries and nuts that could be sold if people would gather them. "You will have to learn where they are. You will have to work to get them. The trouble with these niggers is they are too afraid to get out of town."

When we got to Shakerag hollow we went to the

stream. There was lots of coon tracks. Grandpa clipped the wings of the birds and tied their feet to their limbs so they could only stand still. He set the traps under them. We went home. I was thinking about everything he had done.

That night Grandpa washed and skraped herbs. He stewed some. All evening he didn't talk at all.

Next morning we went back to Shakerag hollow. Every trap had caught two possums and two coons. The birds were gone. He put the coons and possums in a sack, after he killed them. He said "This is all the game I can use, so we will take the traps in."

We climbed to the top of the canyon where the horse was tied. We scented what Grandpa called a polecat. I ask: "What does it look like?" He said: "It is a good thing to keep away from. It is no good for man nor beast." I had no idea that the polecat would be my most profitable game in the future.

He was in good spirits that day. He said: "You know, I have two sons and two daughters." I can't explain this because I was not his son. He didn't like me to call him Grandpa. I had to call him Papa. I suppose it was because I carried his name: Green. I didn't carry my white family name. He never called me Ely. As far back as I can remember he called me Red Horse. My little brother was dark, so he called him Black Horse. We were like a team of horses. My brother always called him Grandpa but not me. Aunt Ada's daughter, Trudy, was a bastard, and she had to call him Papa, too.

As we rode through the woods he was humming. He

said: "Red Horse, you know Mat is coming to Sewanee next week. I can't keep you with me unless you don't want to stay with her. I will miss you. We have had a lot of fun. That is something I don't have much of. My wife told me last night that Mat's youngest son has got married. Mat is going to live with them in a house out by the graveyard." I said nothing.

As we came to the road, he ask: "Do you want to live with her?" I said: "Yes, Papa. She needs me." He said: "Times is hard with this panic on. She won't find it easy to live like it has been. These white people are not helping the nigger like they have been." I said: "They will help us, Papa. I know Father Gerry will." He said: "They are having a hell of a time taking care of themselves."

He said: "I got to stop at Jack Prince house for a few minutes. I want him to come and look at one of my cows that won't eat." Prince was somewhat of a vetinarian, a bounty-hunter and a deputy. I had seen him many times. We stopped in front of the house. Jack Prince came to the door, and yelled: "You old polecat. What are you doing over here? Come on in."

I waited on the horse. Soon a boy drove up with a yoke of oxen and a load of wood. He was about two years older than I. He stopped in front of the house, and began unloading the wood. He said: "Ain't that horse old Ned's?" I said: "Yes. Who are you?" He said: "I am Henry Prince. Jack is my daddy. I guess Ned stopped to have a drink. He and Pa is big chums. Pa looks after his stock."

When he finished unloading, he said: "Come on in. Ned will be here for a while." I went in with him. I liked him, the way he acted so sure of himself. He talked like he was a man. Jack and Grandpa was having a nip, sitting in front of the fireplace.

Mrs. Prince came to the door of the kitchen. She looked at me, asking Henry: "Who is the boy?" Henry said: "He is old Ned's grandson." She said: "You boys come in the kitchen and get some food." At first I refused. She said: "Wouldn't you like some gingerbread and sasfras tea?" I couldn't refuse that.

I just couldn't stop looking at her. She was pretty with her black eyes, black hair, and dark complexion. And so very kind. She was not like the other women of the sager class. There were many guns around the house, and I looked at them.

Jack and Grandpa were looking at me and smiling. Grandpa said: "Jack, that boy is going to be just like me. He's going to be a mountain man. I am teaching him to know all about herbs and how to trap." Jack said: "He couldn't have a better teacher. Ned, I don't believe there is anything that you can't catch. When are you going to bring me a coon?" Grandpa said: "It is out there on the horse." We went out to get the coon.

I rushed ahead, pulled the sack off the horse, and untied it, dumping the coons and possums out. Jack taken the smallest coon.

I said to Mr. Prince: "We killed a coon the other night that weighed twenty-two pounds. It liked to have drowned the dogs." Grandpa told the story how he had to go in the water and throw the coon out. He said: "Red Horse is still thinking about it." Jack said: "There isn't anything this old polecat don't know. I will teach you to shoot. A good mountain man must be a good shot. Ain't that right, Ned?" Grandpa said: "Yes. He is gun crazy." Jack slapped Grandpa on his back, and said: "I will be at your house at four o'clock to look at that heifer." We started for home.

I ask Grandpa: "Why does Jack have so many guns?" He started telling me that Jack Prince was often made a deputy of law when any of the mountaineers got bad and killed somebody. There would be a price on the man's head. Jack would go and get him only when it was "dead or alive". He was a tough mountain man, and the best shot anywhere around.

Grandpa said: "He has had gun battles many times. He has got men that the sheriff didn't want to tackle. I can't call him a sager like the rest of the poor white trash. He is betwixt-and-between the sager and the high-up white people. He is one of my best friends and he is all man."

As we rode on I was thinking: "They didn't say Negro or bastard at any time. This man I must take as a friend. He will teach me how to shoot. That is what I want to learn most of all, so I won't have to take nothing off of anybody. I will work and buy the best gun that can be bought."

Jack came as he promised. He examined the cow. They gave her a drench.

When they finished, I got my air gun. I ask Mr. Prince to tell me how I should shoot. He said: "There are many things to learn about shooting. First, you must learn to head a target." He showed me. "Don't pull the trigger when you are heading. Squeeze the shot off. When you get good at that I will teach you more—like shooting quickly from the hip. By the time you are seventeen you should be good.

Your nerves are very good, and you are quick. It takes that to be a hunter of men or animals." He got on his horse, saying: "You are welcome at my house anytime."

I stood looking after him, wondering why he had called Grandpa a polecat. He was a fine man. He invited me to his home. I would make him my friend. Everything I wanted to do and know was there for me. I was happier than I had ever been.

Mama Mat would be coming in the next three days, and would bring Tepsy, my dog. I would have a gun and a dog all my own. Soon I would have a gun I could kill game with.

I went to the house. Grandpa was scalding the possums to clean them. I watched him scrape the hair off. How white they became. I just couldn't eat them—they looked too much like a cat. When he finished cleaning them he put them in a flour sack, bent a sapling over, tied them on it, and let it go back up. He would let them stay there for many days before he would eat them.

While we were eating supper, Grandpa said to his wife: "I am having a telephone put in. I am the only nigger in Sewanee that will have a phone. The number is nineteen. When the white people want me, they can call me on my phone."

After supper he started chopping up the herbs. Ever was gazing in a small mirror at her straitened hair. She had carried this mirror constantly for several days. She said: "Ned, we have thirty pounds of butter, and you haven't said one word about my hair. I want a big looking-glass in the house. All I can see in this one is my eyes." Grandpa kinder grunted: "I had better do it before you get that mirror molded in some butter. You look at yourself every fifteen minutes since you got strait hair." I left them sitting before the fire, and went to bed very tired.

Next morning I awaken early. We milked the cows. Then, while we were sawing wood a man drove up—tall and old and black. His hair was white and he had a high hat on. He was driving a flea bitten gray mare with a small spring wagon.

Grandpa said: "Hello, Parson. I haven't seen you since you married Ever and I two years ago. You must have left Beans Creek before day to be here this early." Parson said: "Yes, it takes time to drive nine miles and climb the mountain, too." We went in the house with the Parson.

He said: "I came up here to give my blessing to you all and the baby. Let us pray." We got to our knees. Parson moaned and prayed for at least ten minutes. After he was finished Ever said: "Ned, kill two chickens. Parson is hungry. I will cook right away. He likes chicken."

While they were arranging dinner, I got my air gun and went out to practice. Later, Ever called me to come in. The food was on the table—fried chicken, hot biscuits, peach preserves, fried sweet potatoes. The Parson blessed the table with another prayer.

Parson asked Ned: "Who is the boy?" This was the first time I heard Grandpa say I was his grandson. That's what he told him. Parson said: "Bring him when you-all come down to meeting. In May we will have a big time at the foot-washing. That boy needs to be put in the right path now. Brother Ned, I am very much a lover of King Solomon. He said: Train a tree when it is a sprout. So don't spare the rod on no child."

Parson was still eating after we had finished. He didn't stop until he had ate everything on the table. Grandpa said: "No, I won't bring him. He is an Episcopalian, and a good boy. I don't have to use the rod on him." Parson just grunted.

He started to talk about how hard times were with the panic, and he was compelled to lean on the strong arm of his brothers. Collections were low. No one had any money. "I came to you for some donation. Anything you can spare, I will be gracious to have. I know you have plenty. That's why I was so glad to see this gal marry you. You are a smart man, and a good Christian." This was the first time I had heard anybody call Grandpa a Christian. Ever said: "Sure, Parson we will help."

I could see that Grandpa was getting tired. He said: "Parson, what do you want?" Parson said: "I don't want much. Just enough to keep body and soul together." Just then, someone called for Grandpa—it was the feed man. He had brought feed for the cows. Grandpa said to Ever: "Look after Parson, and give him what he needs. I will be busy for a while putting feed in the barn loft."

Parson praised Grandpa highly to Ever, telling her how lucky she was to have such a good provider. "Now, let me get you fixed up," she said and taken him in the smokehouse where meat was hanging all around the walls. Parson stood staring at the meat. He said: "You are just as pretty as your Ma was when she was young." Ever smiled, and said: "Get what you think you need. Ely will help you take it to the wagon. I have to get back to the baby."

Parson taken four hams and four shoulders off the

wall. Then, two stands of lard and four sides of bacon. He didn't carry one piece. I had to make many trips.

When we got the meat loaded, he went in the house, and ask: "Sister Ever, do you have any bedded vegetables and some butter and eggs?" She told him: "Yes." She taken him to the cellar where there were cabbages, turnips, sweet and Irish potatoes—all bedded in sand and straw. Parson filled two grass sacks full.

I told Parson he would have to help me with the sacks. Ever taken one end of a sack and I the other. Parson just walked to and fro with us. When we got all this on the wagon it was full.

I went to tell Grandpa that Parson was leaving. We started to the Parson's wagon. Grandpa let out his pet word: "God-ding, I didn't tell him to move me away. That wagon will break down before he gets down the mountain."

Parson saw us coming and rushed to meet us. "Brother Ned, your heart is bigger than a horse. I don't know any other that could persuade me to take as I have—only you and your lovely wife. All Christians know that the scripture say: it is better to give than to receive. And you will receive many blessings as a cheerful giver." Parson kept talking as he got on the wagon. He said: "I will be looking for you the second Sunday in May. I must try to be home by dark. It is one o'clock already." He drove down the trail.

Grandpa stood looking after him. Ever went to the house. I knew that Grandpa wasn't pleased at all about Parson taking so much. Parson didn't let Grandpa say a word. He still hadn't said anything after he said: "God-ding." He just stood there looking at Parson going down the trail.

He seemed to be pondering over something for a few minutes. Then, he said: "God-ding if I can get this here religion right, so help me. There is a big man that could plow, cut wood, and raise his own food. Instead he has the nerve to come to a hard-working man's house to take what he wants. This is why I just can't get the Resurrection in my mind. And this talk about the white folks here in Sewanee not being Christians. I don't know if they are or not, but there is one thing they don't do, and that is go to peoples' houses and rob them in the name of God. They are giving instead of taking from us niggers."

Then, he said: "Let's get back to sawing wood. Confound it, if I could get this Resurrection in my head it might be better." We sawed wood until we had enough. Grandpa went in the smoke house to see half of one side of the smoke house cleaned of meat. He said: "God-ding the Communion of Saints."

That evening, while we were eating supper, Grandpa said: "That Parson sure can eat. I thought he would never get that long gut of his full. The reason I wanted Red Horse to come and eat with us was because the Parson never can get enough when chicken is on the table." Ever said: "Ned, you are just mad, just mad because you had to give away something. The things you use to do when you were courting me. You put five dollars in the collecting. You came down there with a rubber-tired buggy and a span of horses. I and the other people thought you were rich."

116

He pushed his chair back from the table, and said: "If this God-ding Parson has to come and bless the baby many times we will be in the poor house. I have to go on my privy work tonight. Keep the fire going when you go to bed. The reason, I suppose, there is no nigger preachers in the Episcopalian churches here is they wouldn't be allowed to beg people or rob them on the word of the scripture."

After a short while Mama Mat's youngest son came to tell me to come next morning to the house that we were going to live in to help him clean it up. He said some sager had been living in it, and it was filthy. Mama Mat was coming two days later.

The house would be close to the cemetary. I was glad. I, like most all Negroes, liked to attend funerals when any of the high-ups died. They all got a military funeral. I liked to hear the shots and taps blown.

Next morning I had to walk a half mile to the house. It was close to where Jack Prince lived. We scrubbed and cleaned the house. It was very dirty. We got moved that afternoon.

I had to go back to Grandpa's that night to sleep. I had to meet the eight o'clock train the next morning. I was so glad my dog will be with Mama. Grandpa said: "Red Horse, I wish you were going to stay with me. I am going to miss you a lot." Ever said: "I will, too."

Grandpa said: "Come and stay once in a while. I will go to the train in the morning and haul trunks for Mat. You can take anything you want with you." I reached over, put my hand on his, and said: "I can't." He said: "If I can give a God-ding preacher everything he wants, I surely can give my son what he needs."

This was sweet music to my ears. I thanked him, and said: "When I am a good mountain man, I will give it back to you." He said: "I know you will. You are too much like me. You won't ever ask for much from any one. You are too brave to use people. I am glad you are made that way."

I had become a bit sentimental. Tears was dropping from my cheeks. I was so happy to have someone to love me. I hadn't felt like this since I left Ann who was far away in Texas. I loved her dearer than anyone.

That night I lay in bed thinking: "Almost three years now and no one has called me a bastard or a clabber. I am grown up. I am fifteen. I don't have to take anything I don't like off of anybody. I will fight when I am misused. That's what Grandpa or Jack Prince would do. I am a bastard I know, but I don't like to be reminded of it. I won't be a nigger or a Negro from the way the law treats them. They are not free men. I am going to be a man. A Negro is not a man except with other Negroes. When white men speak to Negroes they bow. I don't see why, brave as Grandpa is, everytime one of them speaks to him he pulls his hat off and bows way down. I guess that's why they call him good old Ned. He is good. Lots of Negroes call him a devil or a pole-cat. I don't like that name at all. They don't know him."

CHAPTER

8

The next morning we met the train. Grandpa and I loaded the trunk on the wagon. Mama Mat scolded me for not staying in Winchester and going to school. I thought I was going to get a whipping. Aunt Charlotte was with her. They got in the wagon. Tepsy, my dog, was so glad to see me he chewed my hand and whined as if he was trying to talk. I refused to ride. I wanted to walk with my dog. We taken a short cut and beat them home. I stopped by my stepfather's house and got the fourteen dollars he was keeping for me.

I had noticed that Mama Mat was criploing badly, and was in a bad humor. Aunt Charlotte's knees was as large as her head, caused from inflamtory rhumatism. I knew how bad Mama need me. School or no school I would take care of her. I started the fire in both stoves.

When they arrived she and Grandpa was quarreling as always. I helped Grandpa get the trunks and bundles in the house while Mama and Aunt Charlotte hobbled inside. Grandpa called me to the wagon before he left, and said: "Red Horse, she need you with her. I see how bad. I am going to bring meat, butter and milk this afternoon."

I went into the house with my air gun in my hand.

Tepsy was still licking my hands—he was so glad to be with me. I had prepared my feelings to take a whipping if that was what it taken to please her. Mama believed in whipping children for anything she thought they done wrong. I had got lots of whippings from her.

They were busy taking their belongings out of the trunk. Mama looked around and saw I had a gun. She said: "Where did you get a gun? And what did you do with your money that you were to go to school on? I am going to to whip the hide off you my little man. I will teach you to do what I tell you to do."

I taken the fourteen dollars from my pocket and gave it to her. "I had fifteen dollars when I got here. I bought two pair of stockings at fifty cents, and I paid fifty cents down on this gun. Mama, if you want me to go back to school I will." Aunt Charlotte looking strait at Mama: "Mat, wasn't that sweet of him to save the money for you? How can you whip him?" Mama looked the other way.

Aunt Charlotte was an educated woman, and had taught school at Stevenson, Alabama. Her husband, Uncle Henry, had died since I left Alabama. He had been one of the tenth cavalry men who charged the block house. He had told me the story many times. He had often said he wished he could educate me.

Aunt Charlotte was holding the barrel of a shotgun in her hand. She said: "This is Henry's gun. I want you to have it when you are sixteen. You have a few months to go. You will have to get someone to put the stock on it because I had to take it off so I could put it in the trunk."

Mama spoke: "I am not going to whip you this time. I don't know if I can spare you to go to Winchester or not."

Aunt Charlotte said: "Mat, I will teach him here. He will be my only pupil." Mama said: "That will be fine. I had forgotton you used to teach school."

Aunt Charlotte said: "Mat, Ely and I have a lot in common that you don't know about. He use to come to me and Henry often to ask questions. The boy studies all the time. Sometimes he gets stalled in his mind. That's when he comes to me to get the explanation. I thought he would go crazy about the Negro religion. I helped him all I could."

Then, she looked at me: "How do you see it now?" I said: "I understand it thoroughly, Aunt Charlotte." She said: "How you have advanced so quick. Did you give up trying to be converted?" I said: "Yes. When I came here to see Father Eastern he explained to me that I am a Christian, but I will never be the shouting kind. I am an Episcopalian. I was born one. I will live as one. Living and loving people will be my job, if I can. Although I just can't see how I can be a Negro. I won't be that."

Mama Mat said: "I don't want to hear any more about you being a Negro." Aunt Charlotte handed me a small dictionary, and said: "Look up Negro." I found the word nigger first. It said: "pertaining to Negro." I closed the book and gave it back to Aunt Charlotte.

I taken the bucket and went to the spring for water. On the way I was thinking how things were summing up: "Everything is coming to me. I am making people love me— even Grandpa. Soon, I will have a real gun all my own. I am close to Father Eastern and close to Jack Prince. He will fix the gun for me. I haven't been called any names for a long time. I am not going to let anybody call me names anymore. I don't care if I don't play with the boys in the bottom. I have plenty to do. I soon will be going into the mountains. No Negroes out there—nothing but sagers. They don't call you names you don't like."

Just as I got to the house Grandpa drove up, calling me to come and help him unload. He brought two hams, two shoulders, a stand of lard, butter, cabbages, turnips, potatoes and sausage. He hung the meat to the rafters on the back porch.

He told Mama: "What money you have, hold on to it. Everybody is using scrip to buy with. You write a note to the Brooks Store and ask for credit, and the Winn Store. They will give you credit. These white people here in Sewanee believe in taking care of us niggers. They ain't gonna let their niggers starve. Not us good ones. These provisions I brought you is not a gift. I owe them to Red Horse. He has worked hard since he came, helping me milk, sawing wood and curing meat. I am paying him off in provisions."

Mama said: "You are trying to be better since you got a seventeen year old wife. I hear she is one pretty country gal. You had better be good to her because I can't raise your daughter like I did Ely's mother thirty years ago. You know you are the meanest polecat to women that ever lived. I think you got trouble on your hands to come. And don't bring it to me. I think any old coot sixty years old trying to match life with a gal seventeen years old is crazy." Grandpa could never out-talk Mama. He just grinned, and said: "Anything you need that I got just let me know."

Mama gave me a note to take to the Brooks Store. Mr. Brooks was a kind man. He lived inside the corporation with a fine family. This was the biggest store in town, and the only one that delivered free. He and his sons ran the store. Bert and Preston were his sons, and he had a beautiful daughter, Miss Amy. They had always been most kind to me and all colored people.

He read the note, and said: "Tell Mat she can have anything she wants." He filled out our order which was for stapels, and I carried it home. I helped Mama put up the quilting frames. Aunt Charlotte had a lot of quilt facing she had pieced. They began quilting them.

Aunt Charlotte said I was ready for the fourth grade. She gave me money to buy books—a reader, a speller, arithmetic, history, geography. I had to study hard my books, and bat cotton for the quilts.

When they finished a quilt, I would go and show it to what few white people of the upper class were still in town. We sold them for two dollars and a half a piece. I sold several. This money helped buy medicine and linements for them.

I became so happy with Aunt Charlotte's teaching. She would read stories to me. She liked to read. The first book she read to me was Ruby Gordan's book *From the Grave*. My Tennessee history told about Daniel Boone and David Crockett. Every word soaked in pertaining to being a mountain man.

For two months I carried wood out of the woods near by, washed the dishes, and made the fires every morning. And I studied my books and batted cotton. This kept me busy.

The weather had been rough. Mama Mat said to me, as spring came forward: "Ely, you have been a good boy.

This is one winter I haven't put my foot in the snow. We are going to raise a garden. We will do some washing and ironing for the white people. I will make salt rising bread, and you can sell it. I know some people that will buy it. You and I will do the washing. Charlotte can sit and iron, and do the ruffles and the pleeting. This summer we can do good." I said: "Mama, I will make a shine-box and shine shoes." This I started to do at once.

School had opened on March fifteenth. The town was alive again. People were on the move. On Sunday mornings I made close to a dollar shining shoes before Sunday School. For a long time no one had called me any of the names that I didn't like. I had forgotten much of the hate. I was some-body. I knew some people loved me. I would help Mama save money. I decided I would go to school even if I had to go to Saint Mary's at Nashville which Father had spoken of.

All of a sudden Aunt Charlotte decided she would go to her home in Alabama. This left Mama and me alone. I built up a number of customers for bread: Mrs. Selden, Mrs. McCrady, Mrs. McMillan, Mrs. Hall, Mrs. Barnwell. They would take two loaves a week at twenty cents a loaf.

Mama was called the best laundress in the town. She specialized in shirt waists, white skirts, underwear for women, and shirts for men. She said that by doing small jobs like this she could make more out of it. The errands kept me busy.

It seemed to me that Sewanee hadn't ever been as beautiful as it was at that time. The tourists was coming in. The streets had carriages of ladies with ruffled parasols and all dressed in white. The hotels were filled with guests. I sold violets and honeysuckle that I collected wild.

Often the guests would pay me ten cents a gallon for water from the ATO spring. This water was supposed to be ninety per cent pure, equal to Vermont water. Many people came to drink the water from the two springs. The Tremlett springs that the Indians had called Rattle snake springs. Both springs flowed from a cave ice cold, and they were as clear as a crystal.

One morning Mama sent me to deliver a package to the Barnwell boarding house for a lady named Smith. As I was waiting for the money, a lady with a small boy ask me would I like to care for her son in the afternoon? Just weekdays. She would pay a dollar a week. I told her I would have to ask my Mama.

Mama Mat said: "That is good pay, and it's close to home. Tommy, my son, and his wife are going to move in with us. Ora, his wife, can help with the clothes. You take it. That's good pay."

Next day I went to work. The little fellow had been afflicted with typhoid fever the summer before, and was still convalesing from this attack. They were from Meridian, Mississippi. They had come to Sewanee for his health. She said, "Mr. Davis will be here later. The boy's name is Sam. Now you be good to him and I will be good to you." I liked the little boy.

Mrs. Davis bought a hammock so we could swing under the shade tree. I had a lot of fun. There were many other children, mostly girls. They sang a lot of songs— School Days, Come, be my Rainbow. All afternoon we played every day.

I would take Sam on my back to play horse with him. I would play galloping. He got a kick out of it. After playing he would be ready to take his afternoon nap. He would sleep in the hammock while I would swing gently. He was soon full of life.

A month later her husband came. He came out with Sam, and said: "You are the boy that takes care of my son. He has improved so much in this mountain air. And you have helped him a lot." I was so glad to hear him say that. Then, he said: "We likes niggers. We have one name Sambo at home, the cook's boy. Sam is crazy about him. There is nothing like a nigger to care for a white child, I bet on it. You all go and play."

I stood looking at him. He said: "Take him." I said: "No, I won't." At this moment Mrs. Davis walked up. I said: "Lady, pay me. I quit." She said: "Sam, what is wrong?" He said: "How much do you owe him?" She said: "A dollar tomorrow. His week will be up." She ask me: "Why are you quitting?" I told her that I wasn't a nigger and I wouldn't work for anybody that called me a nigger.

She started to say something, but he motion his hand, and gave me a dollar. He said: "I have heard how high-collared the niggers are in this town." I went out the back way not thinking what Mama will say about it.

When I got home Mama, her son and his wife were peeling peaches, sitting on the porch. I was still angry. Mama ask me: "What are you doing home? It is early." I told her I quit. "The man called me a nigger, and I am not going to work for anybody that calls me that." Mama said: "You quit?" I said: "Yes, Mama."

She walked to the willow bush, broke a switch off, and said: "You go back to them people, and ask them to take you back. I will tell you when to quit a job. I thought you had got all that nonsense out of your head." I said:

"Mama, I just can't go back." She began whipping me. I continued saying: "I can't, Mama." She stopped whipping for a moment. "I am going to whip you until you go back to the job."

I knew she meant what she said, so I gave her the dollar, and said: "Alright, Mama. I'll go back." She said: "And you do your job well, and forget about being a nigger." As I walked away I felt the welts on my arms and legs. I would rather die than speak to that white man again.

I decided I would leave Mama, and try to live with somebody else. "I can take care of myself. I am not a nigger to nobody. If I was a bit larger I would have shown him how wrong it is to call people what they are not."

I went to my stepfather's house. He hadn't come from work. Sarah, his wife, was home. I told her I wanted to live with them, and why. She said: "He can't take you from Mama Mat." I could wait until he came and talk to him. I ask him could I live with him for a while?

We sat on the doorstep of his house. I knew he loved me as much as he did his own son. He didn't answer me for a while. He sat looking at the ground.

When he spoke, he said: "You know you are not my son. You were given to Mat to raise, that was your mother's wish. We both loved her. If she had lived things would have been lots different. I don't like to see you having such a hard time. I know Mat is doing the best she know. Try to stay with her. You have been a boy hard to understand. I will go to Mat and have a talk with her. You will soon be a man. Then you can choose for yourself."

I ask him did he think I should go to Grandpa? He said: "No. It won't be pleasant there. Ned is having family trouble. He and Ever are separating. He is drinking a lot. It's no place for you. I will go to see Mat as soon as I eat my dinner. You go home." I had no intention of going home.

I went to the playground where I hadn't stopped in five years. My little brother was playing with his pals, and having a good time with all. He was eight years old. His skin was dark. He had a father. I was pleased to think he was not an orphan, not a bastard. What a difference it makes when you are both.

The sun was still high. It was five o'clock. I wanted to be alone for a while. I started to go up on the main street in the corporation. At this time of day lots of the people taken walks, and I loved to watch them. Many of them spoke to me, and I might find something to do to make money.

I was in my bare feet like all boys my age in the summer months. There was a small stream fed by the overflowing cesspools in the corporation. Little children were playing in the sand. They didn't have no shovels, no sand buckets, no kind of tools like the white children had to play with. I had played in this stream when I was a small boy, damming it up, making waterwheels turn as the water flowed over the dam. What fun it was.

These children didn't have anything to play with except their hands. My thoughts went back to my job. Sam had a sand box, rake, shovel, hoe, three sand buckets, and a wheelbarrow. His daddy called me a nigger. I would steal his toys and give them to these poor kids, that's what I would do.

I had to wait until nine o'clock before it would be dark

enough to slip in the yard and not be seen. I had to crawl a hundred yards to reach the sandbox and then crawl back out. I taken everything except the wheelbarrow. I cut the hammock to threads.

I went back to my stepfather's house and hid the toys in the sulky in the yard. Everybody had gone to bed. I did not awake any one. I layed on the porch to rest, and slept until morning. I heard Sarah beating the round steak. I knew they were going to have chicken fried steak and onion gravy for breakfast. I was so hungry.

I went into the kitchen. Sarah said: "Did you go home?" I told her I had slept on the porch all night. "Where is father?" She said: "He has gone to the well to get fresh water, and to take the milk and butter out of the well where we put it to keep cool. You can go home now. Lee went to talk to Aunt Mat last night. I don't think she will whip you this time." She handed me a bowl of bread crumbs to feed the chickens, which I quickly threw to them.

Father came and ask: "What are you doing here so early?" Sarah said: "He slept on the porch last night." He said: "Why did you do that? Don't ever do that again. You go to Mat as soon as you eat breakfast. And be a good boy. Mat thinks she is right. She said you are getting very hard to handle. She wants you to know how to work. She says people that don't like to work will steal. And we don't want you to be like that."

I went home as I promised. Mama was very angry with me. She didn't whip me. I told her I would find work enough to make seventy five cents a week, if I had time to look for work.

That afternoon I taken the toys I had stolen to the little colored children. There was twice as many as the day before. I didn't have enough toys to go half way around. Some of them began to cry because I hadn't given them any.

Now I was sorry I had brought any. I must do something for the others. So, I raided every playground in the corporation until all the little children had some toys. The idea came to me that white people had everything: they could afford to be stolen from. Negroes had nothing: I was helping them. They will like me for it.

I got a job at Mrs. Emma Tucker's, washing the pot vessels for fifty cents a week and my meals. I would shine the boarders' shoes for five cents a shine. Soon I was making a dollar and a quarter a week. I held this job until school closed for the winter.

One of Mrs. Tucker's daughters was married to a man name Ellery Huntington who was a professor in a college up North. He came South for his vacation in the summer. He became a victim of slow fever and was a bed patient for six months. He forgot how to walk.

Mrs. Susie Huntington, his wife, hired me, after the students had left, to stay around to keep the coal supply in. I soon became his nurse. I taught him to walk again.

I was the only one for a while that could persuade him to take his medicine, and eat what his diet call for. I would sit on the bed, and plead with him to eat. He would say: "Ely, you sure want me to get well, don't you?" He would take a mouthful and hold it before he could swallow it, as if it was repulsive. Sometimes tears would be rolling down my cheeks by the time he finished.

He began to gain rapidly in January, 1909. One morning Dr. Hall called me and Miss Susie into the hall to try to get him to walk. This was the hardest task we had to do—Mrs. Huntington on one side and I on the other. For two weeks it was a struggle to get him in motion.

Soon he gained his equilibrium and was on his way to health. I massaged him every day. This was my first lesson on being a trainer and practical nurse. By Spring he had gained thirty five pounds.

In May he left for New York. He had two sons: Ellery, Jr. and Fritz. I never saw him again. Fifty three years later I did see Mrs. Susie Huntington again.

For six months no one had mentioned nigger nor bastard at all. I had about forgotton it. The only time I saw any colored people was Sunday afternoon when I went to Sunday school. No one ever insulted anybody there.

This year, 1909, everything taken a big change. St. Augustus got a new presider by the name of Tyson, a minister from New York. Father Gerry went to South Carolina where he was made Bishop. The school changed from summer sessions to winter sessions like all other colleges in the South. The medical and law schools were relinquished. Four training classes remained: theology, civil engineering, military academy, and arts & sciences.

We colored people had a good go. School all winter and tourists all summer. All table-waiting, pressing, cooking, janitor work, and most of the dray business was done by colored people. A good laundress could make more money than anybody.

This is when I became to know how the white people were interested in the progress of their colored people. We

131

had football teams and baseball teams. The coaches of varsity teams would come and coach our teams. Any colored college that would come to play with us they would invite them. White people would attend the games.

We had two dance halls. All college boys got the hotel work at Monteagle, another resort six miles away. Sewanee was the favorite headquarters for them to come to. To me at that time Sewanee was a little Rome of the South.

This year I taken a vast change from loving everybody and trying to love everybody. I was struck harder in insults and imposed on willfully more than ever before. I was almost seventeen, and a bit small to be my age.

One morning, as I was returning from delivery of laundry, a wagon of sagers came through the corporation. I ask could I ride? One of them nod his head. I climbed in from the back. Just as I straightened up I saw the larger one standing with a hand ax drawn back to throw. He said: "No nigger rides in my wagon." He threw the ax. I could not dodge it. It struck me in the chest, knocking me unconscious out of the wagon in front of the Gregory home.

When I came to my senses Mrs. Gregory and her son had dragged me out of the road to the sidewalk. Wiping my face with a wet towel, she said: "You are Ely. I saw that man throw the ax. How evil can anyone be? Can you walk?" My chest was hurting very bad. She said to her son: "Help him go to Dr. Joe Selden's." The doctor said I had a fractured collarbone. When he finished setting it, he said I would have to wear the bandage for two weeks.

I was very bitter, thinking what white people will do to a colored person. "I am going to be like the Negroes in Alabama. Keep me a gun. This is the last time that any white person will ever harm me again that I don't do it back. I will get even with this sager some day, if I have to shoot him."

When I got home I told Mama Mat how it happen, but I didn't tell her my thoughts of revenge. Mama only said: "Keep off other peoples' wagons. You had no right to ask for a ride from people you don't know. They must be some sagers from Tick Bush. They are all mean, and don't like Negroes. I am glad the blade didn't strike you."

I had carried the ax home with me—it was very sharp —and I was to carry this ax in the mountains with me for three years.

For weeks I could barely walk around. I went to the playground where the colored kids played. No one had anything to say to me. They acted as if I wasn't there.

One day I taken my dog and went to Morgan Steep look-out. I went to the herb beds where Grandpa had show me every thing green and fragrant. I recognized gensand with the red flower in the fork of the stalk like Grandpa told me it would be, growing in the shade of the muscadine vines.

I sat at the waterfall for a long time, thinking for the first time about life—what is to be done with life. "Some people have everything. Others don't have anything and have to be kicked around." I thought of everything I felt that was wrong that had been done to me.

It seemed that everybody of the Negroes and poor white people wanted to hurt anybody they could. "This is why I am being treated like I am. Nobody cares for me. The aristocrats have been good to me because they know they are the cause of me being a bastard. My Uncle and my

Grandmother don't ever say anything to me. I must find something to do that I don't have to bother them." Every bitter thought I had ever had came back.

Tepsy, my little fox terrier, was looking me in my face as if he understood everything I was thinking. He put his head in my lap, and lay there. I made up my mind this would be last time I would ever be humble to anybody. "I will fight anybody that do me wrong—Negroes and white people. Father Eastern tells me to love everybody. This would be alright if somebody loved me."

I began to pray asking to be shown what to do and how. I lay back on the rock, looking into the sky. It was pleasant and warm on this rock.

Suddenly, I was talking to my Mama Lena. I thought she was standing by me. She was saying: "Be brave, my son, be patient. Go up and look at the beauty in God's mountains." Tepsy was still lying with his head in my lap. I knew it was a dream. I had to sit and think it over for while. It seemed so real that she was there.

We climbed to the top of Morgan Steep. I remembered she said look at God's mountains. When I looked out over the caldron I noticed the laurel was in bloom. The whole ridge to the right was crimson red. I stood gazing at how beautiful it was. There were magnolia trees with huge white blossoms flickering in the sun like the wings of a flock of white birds. I sat down to look at this beautiful sight from the mountain of God.

The sound of Cannon Ball as it reported at Cowan floated up the canyon and added to the enchantment. I could almost hear the mountains say: "This is where you belong. I will take care of you." I stayed there until the sun set. This added more beauty to the scene. Many people came, walking and in carriages. I did not even look to see who they were.

I had found the answer to what I wanted to know. These mountains were my home. They belonged to God. I rose and started home in soft twilight. Something had happened that day that I did not try to tell anybody about.

CHAPTER

9

When I got home Mama Mat asked where I had been gone all day. I told her of the day and how peaceful things had been, and that I had been in an unusual good humor. She smiled and said: "What will you think of next?"

Then, she said: "That was the Newby boy that hit you with the ax. Jack Prince told me today. They are some of the Tick Bush sagers. Jack said you should come out to see him." I said: "It is alright, Mama. I'll get even with him if he stays on these mountains. I am not going to let no one get by with nothing. Nobody. Niggers or white people. When they hurt me I am going to hurt back."

Mama Mat said: "You shut up. You will get killed making trouble with white people, even if they are sagers." I had started to the kitchen to go to bed. Why I felt so sure of myself I don't know. I had never said anything back contrary to her opinion before tonight.

I stopped in the doorway. "Mama, you can whip or kill me if you should want. I won't raise my hand against you. But no one had better put a hand on me to hurt me—not even your son will whip me again. No one except you."

Mama ask: "What's come over you today? Who have you been talking to?" I said: "No one except the mountains and Mama Lena. I can see people will keep you on your

136

knees if you will stay there. I am not that blood. I guess I am not a nigger. He has no law and is not even a man. I am going to be a man. I am going to take care and protect you and everything I have." She just stood looking at me when I said good night.

That night as I lay in bed I wasn't sleepy. I had slept on the rocks a long while. I thought of my Mama Lena— how she linger with her sickness that was incurable. "I hope I don't have to die with consumption. I will do as Dr. Selden says I should to keep from having it. Some people claim it is heretitary. I am small to be my age. I must develop and be strong. Dr. Joe will tell me how to do it."

Next day I went to see Dr. Selden. He told me that consumption was not inheiritted. It was contracted. Sleeping out of doors was good. Never sleep closed in. With plenty of fresh air you should never have it. He showed me how to take breathing exercises and how to do athletic work. I should never smoke cigarettes.

When I left him I stopped at Mrs. Gregory's house to thank them for aiding me when I was hurt. Her sons had a glass of lemonade each. She gave me a glass, too.

Mrs. Gregory said: "Ely, I need someone to empty the slop jars and fill the water pitchers in my rooms every evening. Would you do this? I will pay twenty five cents a week." I agreed to do it because it was close to home. I could do it anytime between two o'clock and six in the afternoon.

I went to Jack Prince's house when I left the Gregorys. I knew I wanted to see Jack Prince more than anyone I knew. When I arrived at his house, he yelled out: "Come, little Ned." I went in the house.

He said: "I am going out to the barn. How is your

shoulder? Those Tick Bush sagers are a hell of a lot. Don't ever have any part of them polecats. Boy, you ought to go around old man Ned more often. He is drinking himself to death. That young wife is driving him crazy. I found him lying on the ground drunk the other morning out there in the woods with his privy wagon. I did not tell Mat. I know how you think of him. He is a good old polecat and thinks a lot of you. So, go and see him."

He walked toward the barn. He was still talking about Grandpa. A man drove up name Dodson. I knew he often sold produce from the valley. He leaped off the wagon, snatched out a pistol, and drew on Jack, saying: "I got you this time." My heart almost choked me. I didn't know they were friends. I thought it was the real thing.

Jack said: "Where did you get it, Dodson?" He said: "I bought it off a skunk for ten dollars." He handed the gun to Jack, saying: "It's one of the latest. It's a Colt forty-five." Jack said: "What balance!" He threw a tin can into the garden twenty steps away. For six shots he kept the can bouncing.

Dodson said to me: "He is the best the country has got." Jack said to Dodson: "This is my pupil. He is going to be a mountain man. You ought see him shoot a damn air gun. He don't miss a dime twenty feet away. I only gave him one lesson. That was how to squeeze the shot off. He hold a gun like his arms were made of stone. He don't have any nerves. I am going make him the best rifle man around here. You'll see."

Dodson said: "If we have to stop a feud like we had with the Tick Bush bunch that time we will need him." Jack said: "Don't mention that." They laughed, as Dodson got on his wagon and drove away. Jack said: "Dodson and I have had some tough jobs rounding up the moonshiners in these mountains."

I said: "Mr. Prince, I want a rifle, a good one—a Winchester that is good for a hundred yards." He said: "What the hell are you going to shoot that far away?" I said: "That's what I want." He said: "You are not thinking of shooting somebody, are you?" I said: "If that has to be done, that's it." Jack said: "You stick close to me. I'll do your fighting. I know you are bitter towards some people. But forget about fighting."

Henry, his son, drove up: "You are just who I want to see. How would you like to work with me this winter? I have leased five hundred acres of railroad tie cutting. I have a contract for three sets of switch ties and two strait sets. I am to deliver them in March. I will pay you fifty cents a day. We will hue the ties where we cut the trees and snake them out with the oxen. You can learn to drive them. When we don't want to work we will hunt."

I didn't answer him at once. Jack said: "If you will help him, I will let you have a gun—a Winchester thirty-two special. You will have to leave it here. You will have it only when you are going to hunt. You can't shoot it around town. The range is too far. I want eight dollars for it. You can pay fifty cents a week. It's a good gun—trued to the finest bead. In a few days you will be picking the eyes out of woodpeckers."

I told him I had to ask Mama. Jack said: "Mat won't care. She knows I will take care of you at all times."

On the way home I passed the graveyard, and saw Cretcher and Henry Woods digging a grave. I knew some notable had died and there was to be a big funeral. I hadn't been up-town since I was hurt. I hadn't heard that Mr. DuBose had died. Henry Woods told me.

I felt somewhat sick for a few moments. I had known him from the first day I was large enough to be on the streets. He always spoke to me. When he was at a distance he would motion his cane at me like a salute.

I knew this would be a military funeral. I would have to see it. I had to wait an hour. While I was waiting two white boys came. They did not go over in the main streets where most of the other boys played, and I would only see them on Sunday at church when I went to see the cadets parade. I knew they were of the notables that lived in the corporation. They had been hunting.

Each spoke to me. One boy was seventeen, the other was my age. They told me their names were D. S. and John McKay. D. S. was the oldest, and had a twenty-two calibre rifle. He said: "Let's go over back of the graveyard and target practice while we wait for the procession."

I told them my intention of becoming a mountain man, and about the profit that could be made if you just knew where to find it: herbs, berries, nuts, grapes, flowers, mineral water, and game of all kind. "I am studying how to be a crack shot." John was most interested in my plans.

They found a small tin can and placed it against the rock wall. Each of them taken turns shooting at it. Four shots each—no hits. D. S. ask me did I want to try? I said: "Yes, but I haven't shot a real gun like this one. I only have an air gun." He handed me the gun. I only knew how to shoot with one hand. He cocked the gun for me. I shot five times, hitting the can every shot.

140

They were astounded to find that I could beat them, shooting with one hand. I explained everything Jack had taught me. Here I had found a hunting partner.

We decided to get on the rock fence close to the gate where we could see the procession. The fence was five feet high. They helped me get up on the fence, and put my dog on it to. We sat there through all of the ceremony. This was an unusual day for me.

I could see people coming from all directions. I saw my Grandfather and ten other older Negroes. Most of them were so-called Uncles. They went in among the white people. When I looked again they had been placed at the head of the grave. There they stood with their bald heads shining in the afternoon sun. I knew that they had come to pay their respects to a great man that had been their friend. I knew the white people at Sewanee held a high appreciation of their loyalty.

I had already become to feel sentimental when the cadets marched in. They were so proud as they executed their comands so gracefully. My attention went to Grandpa, cleaned up with a black suit on. I knew he would have his most confusing thoughts—The Communion of Saints, the Resurrection, and the blessing which he always said—A man borned of a woman is in this world only a few days, and his heart is filled with trouble." I wondered if it could be that he thought that phrase was correct because the earth was being fed back its own. I always tried to find some way to make Grandpa right.

Soon the cadets fired the shots of salute. Then, taps were blown. My mind went back to when I was seven years old and the cadets were my pride and joy. I was a bit sad.

D. S. asked me would I walk home with them? It was only three hundred yards away. I was glad to do so. I knew I had found friends in them. D. S. introduced me to his mother. Johnny began to tell her what friends we were to be. This boy become the best friend I had for four years. His mother treated me as if I were part of the family. Soon we would begin to hunt together. Mrs. McKay gave us some lemonade.

Next morning I went to Dr. Selden's. He removed the brace from under my arm, and taped my shoulder with adhesive so I could put my arm through the sleeve of a coat. I went home, and ask Mama: "Could I have fifty cents to get a hat to wear Sunday?"

It has been four years since I had gone to Saint Augustus to see the cadets march in. I knew I would see many people that I used to know. I had seen Father Gerry at the cemetery. He had come to preside over the ceremony out of respect for this great man.

I told Mama about the McKays. She didn't know them. They hadn't lived in Sewanee very long. I rarely wore a hat in the summer. I explained to Mama the reason I wanted a hat was I could tip my hat like the men. I would not have to bow. She smiled and shook her head with a shrug of her shoulders. Things had changed in every way since I had felt adopted by the mountains. I never talked to anyone about this—except Tepsy.

All day Saturday I planned what I would do to start to make money. Wild grapes were ready. Lots of people bought them, and muscadine. I could make at least a half dollar a day. What I couldn't sell Mama could use. Hunting grapes, Johnny and I could locate walnuts, hickory nuts and chestnuts which we could sell to the school boys. The school boys were fond of nuts, and would buy all we could gather. We would gather herbs, too. I would tell Johnny about it.

Sunday morning I put on my suit I had bought to go to school, the first new suit I had owned. I had to go in bare feet as I didn't have any dress shoes. The August sun was bright and hot. I got to Saint Augustus before anyone except the janitor, who also pumped the pipe organ. I wanted to see the notables as they drove up in their carriages.

Soon D. S. and Johnny arrived. People were coming from all directions, some walking, some in carriages. Ladies were nearly all dressed in white with parasols. Many used rented carriages, called hacks, mostly owned by Henry Hoskins. We watched the carriages drive up and unload.

I was hoping to see Vice-Chancellor Wiggins drive up because he had the finest span of horses—he and also Professor Gray. They only lived a half-block from the church. I saw Mr. and Mrs. Wiggins as they crossed the street. Like most all the notables he carried a walking stick, his silk hat glittering in the sun.

By this time the street was full of people. Every one was greeting one another. A carriage stopped beside us that gave me a joyful thrill—it was a lady I admired, Miss Sallie Malhado, whom I hadn't seen in three years. She and Lady Gallier was riding in her carriage. She was the type of lady that made her presence felt wherever she appeared. I stepped forward catching the reins close to the horse's bridle. Mr. Calmore, who most of the students called General,

143

his two daughters, Miss Dora and Miss Eva, with Miss Hodson walked up. He assisted the two ladies out of Miss Sallie's carriage.

After their greetings Miss Malhado looked to see who was holding her horse. She said: "Why, Ely, you little scrapper. I haven't seen you for a time. Take the weight out of the buggy. Snap the strap to the horse." This was something I had done for her when I was a small boy and she would drive up to the supply store.

Miss Sallie was always busy like most of that class of people. She was a brave woman. She drove her horse like any man could. She often would drive into the colored settlement to see about people that was sick, driving her carriage over ditches and rough roads. Many times when she would be going in my direction she would stop her horse and tell me to get in the carriage. She would drop me off where it was most convenient for me. She was a great lady like all of those people.

The Kirby Smiths drove up—Miss Bessie and Miss Carry, the Smith sisters, the remainder of General Kirby Smith's family. They had a colored butler that the General had raised from a small boy. His name was Ed, and he was said to be the finest butler in town. He was treated like one of the family. The two ladies mostly drove for themselves, using a one seat carriage. But, this day Ed had to go with them to help keep them from wrinkling their dresses. The gentlemen helped them from their buggy, and Ed stayed to care for the horses.

The cadets were approaching about a block away, so Johnny and I got in Miss Malhado's carriage to see over the crowd. That was to me the most wonderful sight to look at. It was the most regrettable experience for me when I learned I could never be a cadet. Here they came—a column of individual human beings swaying with synchronize motion, keeping caden with the music of the band—coming to give their respect to God.

Johnny touched me on the arm, and said: "Two years from now I will be a cadet." This was a time I found that I envied Johnny, and I did not answer him. He said: "This is a new uniform they are wearing. It's like the West Point cadets."

Very few people had gone in the chapel. Most of the people were fond of their cadets. As the cadets marched by us I saw an officer that I knew. He had once been a cadet. I hadn't seen him for many years. He was dressed different than the cadets in a blue coat, gray pants with yellow stripes, a spreaded eagle on his cap, medals on his breast, a silver leaf on his shoulder. I knew he was a high ranking military officer. He and Captain Gillem had marched in front of the cadets, and he gave the command that formed company front.

Then, they filed off two abreast, marching into the chapel. Everybody proceeded after them. Johnny ask me was I going in? I said: "No. You go. I will be in front when you come out." Johnny went with his brother and I rushed to the back of the chapel where the choir assembled to march in with the officials.

There were many visiting Bishops. Bishop Gailor was there—the last time I saw him. I always felt these men had to be next to God. It was beautiful to look at them in their gowns—some black, some purple with white carters and decorated stoles, representing their significance to divinity.

When they marched in I went to the street to look at the horses and carriages. All were driven by colored men, except one—Professor Gray, who had the only white servant in Sewanee that worked around the estate.

Many colored butlers on the street that worked in homes nearby had taken a chance to see the gathering, all of them neatly dressed. It was much encouraged by the notables that their servants be immaculate at all times. You rarely saw any servant on the street without a tie on.

I came upon Mrs. Gillem's carriage. There sat Mamy Gillem, setting and waiting for Mrs. Gillem to return. She didn't go in the chapel as usual, maybe because there was too much of a crowd for her. Her white hair was gathered to the top of her head with a small turban. With her brown skin and her large eyes she was sitting in a dignified way, as if she was a queen. At that time I could almost worship the so-called black Mamy.

I went to Miss Malhado's carriage and sat there until the service was over. There were many students on the premises that could not get in the chapel.

Along came a fine looking big strong black man, the father of a small child I had given some of the toys I stole from the white children. He was the only person that knew I stole from the white children. He was the only person that knew I was stealing, and was the cause of me stopping. He stopped and ask me was I trying to be a good boy? He said: "I am now top trainer for the varsity team. Saturday afternoon, if you will come to the gymnasium, you can get some shoe-shining to do."

His name was Willie, but the students called him Six. A number of them chatted a bit with him about the coming team. When they subsided, I ask him: "Why do they call you Six?" He laughed: "It's because I have big feet. They give me so many shoes, and I can't wear any of them. They kid me by saying I wear size twelve. For short, I am Six." He was as humorous as he was lovable to know. Little did I expect that he would serve for forty years as one of the finest trainers of any college in the South.

Some of the people had began to come out of the chapel. I went close to see everybody when they came out. Johnny and D. S. was already out on the steps. We stood back a distance on the lawn. D. S. said: "They are going to build a new church. This is what this is all about. There is going to be a cornerstone laying next Spring. It will be called All Saints. That excavating over there is where it is going to be."

We were standing just off the walkway on the lawn. Everybody going in that direction would have to pass by us, and the cadets who were last to come out. This day the cadets stole the show. Most of the notable men stood across from us. The cadets went into fast marching and marched by them.

There was an officer with an odd uniform—Major Archibald Butt. He had been a cadet when he was in school, and remembered I had seen him before. He had become to be President Teddy Roosevelt's bodyguard, and right hand man. As the cadets marched by the command was given eyes right. Major was standing out from the rest of the crowd, and this was a respect to him.

When they had marched out the people came into the walkway greeting the visiting guests.

The Bishops were standing on the steps with many

ministers, and many people were greeting them. I went up to shake hands with Bishop Gailor. I hadn't been close to him since I was four years old, when I was baptized. He knew who I was, and grasped my hand gently with his right, and patted the back of it with his left. He said: "God bless you."

I was having a hard time trying to keep my toes from being stepped on. When I got clear of the mass of greeters to the Bishops I was in the middle of the walkway where Major Butt was standing, as people were greeting him. I was trying to recall where did I ever see him? Just then, I realized he was the officer of the cadets when I used to try to keep up with them on Sunday mornings.

I stood looking up at him, my hat in my hand. Close to him were many young ladies: Miss Johnny Tucker, the Kirby Smith ladies, Miss Dora Calmore, Miss Sarah Hodson, and also Frank Gailor, the Bishop's son. They saw me standing back of the Major, staring at him.

Frank said: "Major, you have an admirer." He nodded his head toward me. Major turned, looked at me, and said: "Ely." Then, he extended his hand, and said: "I would know that sandy, curly head anywhere." He lead me to the ladies, and said: "This is the youngest cadet I ever knew. He will be a military man some day. When he was very small he used to march with us on Sunday mornings. He had to run to keep up." I was so burdened with sentimentality that I was petrified. I just couldn't speak.

Mr. Hodson, who ran the bank, Miss Sarah Hodson's brother, taken the Major by the arm and they walked away with the young ladies. I watched them as they crossed the street and entered the Hodson's broad driveway leading to the estate.

It had become one o'clock. Everybody in Sewanee went to dinner at that hour. I told Johnny I would see them the next day and they departed for home.

Miss Malhado and a number of her set were in a group, talking. I was glad to see that she had not gone, as I wanted to hold the horse and put the hitch weight back in her buggy for her. Soon she came with another lady, and Dr. Hall assisted them into the carriage. I had put the weight in, and was holding Joe, the horse, by the reins.

She thanked Dr. Hall, and then said to me: "Ely, you have been most kind looking after me." She held out her hand and dropped a quarter in mine. I bowed, and thanked her. She smiled, and said to the other lady: "Ely is an aristocrat."

I was hungry, and decided to go to Mrs. Emma Tucker's where I was always welcome like most all colored people she knew.

On the way I was thinking how Miss Sallie had said I was an aristocrat. I felt very proud to think that even if I was not white, I was somebody. You have to be somebody to be an aristocrat. I would ask Father Eastern just what an aristocrat is, and why.

At the Tucker house was many people. She had extra help for the day, and for the help and colored people a table was set under a big oak tree. I went to the cook, Eleanora, and ask her: "Could I be of help to you?" She said: "Oh Lord, yes." She tossed an apron to me: "Clean up the pot vessels and empty those slop cans in the back. Your Grandpapy isn't here today. You can do his job." Half an hour later I had finished the job.

She gave me a plate of food, saying: "You can eat now. Heaven knows when we will finish feeding this crowd."

I was hoping it would be fried chicken and candy-yam potatoes which it was, and also peach ice cream. I stuffed myself on ice cream. I told Eleanora that I thank her, and left on my way to Sunday school.

As I was leaving, I met Mr. and Mrs. Rosborough coming into the grounds. He called to me. I went with my hat in my hand like I had seen Grandpa do. He said: "You are growing up to be a fine looking boy. Some day I want you to be my houseman. Do you belong to the choir at your church?" I told him: "Yes." He ask: "What night do you practice?" I told him that Professor Sharp who trained the Saint Augustus choir trained us on Friday night.

He said: "Good. I want you to escort my wife on Thursday nights to her bridge club. That night I am always very busy. I don't like her to be on the street alone. There often are these sagers going through the corporation to the valley. I just don't trust them. I will pay you fifty cents each night. Be at my house Thursday evening at seven o'clock."

He ask what was wrong with my shoulder? I told him what happen. He said: "This poor white trash is a bad lot." The Mrs. smiled, and said: "I will be looking for you." Then she said to him: "You mean to give me a good looking boy-friend." She pulled her parasol back as he gave her a kiss. They went into the grounds.

I would have almost all I could do. I could make

money every day in some way. On my way to Sunday school I thought how the Sewanee people were so different from white people in other towns. "They don't trust their own race. To them I am a Negro. They trust Negroes more than their own poor white people. I am called an aristocrat. This must mean being very good. I will do everything I can to be of good."

As I started down the hill I found Dr. West pushing his small auto up the hill. I ran to help him. This was the first automobile that was owned by anyone in Sewanee. It was called a Brush. It had one cylinder. Not having much power it could not climb the hill with him in it. He had to put it so the clutch could move it, then push it to help the engine until it was on top, then outrun it, and get in.

I helped him up the hill. He was going to the village on a call which was close to my chapel, so he taken me with him.

Nearly all the Bishops and visiting ministers came. This day I was made crossbearer of the choir.

Many white people came to our chapel. They spent much time talking to we colored people. There were lectures given by many of the ministers. When service was over we all walked through the corporation, a habit of us to show respect to our superiors of divinity. Many of the white people would be walking in the afternoon sun. It was a custom with them to speak to every one of us.

I have heard them say to their servants and to other colored: "How nice you looked Sunday." This, of course, was to encourage every colored person to look his best and to be as immaculate as he could. Most of our clothes were second handed. With seven hundred men students, most of them rich mens' sons, the cost of second handed clothes was cheap. This kept every colored man well-dressed.

The white people were very proud of their colored servants. I have heard them—even the school boys—criticize the poor sagers for the way they look. They wouldn't even speak to them.

Scandal was somthing you never heard about the white people. They had everything under such control that if a schoolboy was expelled no one knew why. All you knew was—"He's gone."

That day, as we approached the street where the hotel was, there were many carriages in the street and many ladies walking. It seemed everyone spoke to some of us.

Most of our procession was young people ranging from ten years old to twenty. No older colored people attended Sunday school. I knew the boys and girls would go to Morgan Steep. There they would watch the sunset set —like the tourist do nowadays. Then, they would walk back home in the twilight. This was a remantic place to be at that hour of the day.

I had walked with three of the Fathers. As we reached the supply store they left us to go in the store. I followed them to the steps. I said to one of them: "Father, will you please tell me what an aristocrat is?" He looked at the other two, and smiled: "A man of character, a person who stands for virtue." I thanked him, and joyned the other boys.

CHAPTER
10

I was happy to have a friend like Johnny McKay, who wanted to go with me in the mountains.

Now that I had been selected to be a bodyguard for Mrs. Rosborough maybe other ladies would hire me, and I could make some money every day.

Mrs. Beasley ask me to sell chocolate fudge and crullers at the games on Saturday at the park. She would give me a fourth of what I made. Most Saturdays I made one dollar and a quarter for myself. This selling made me popular with all the students.

Johnny and I would go into the mountains three days a week, and we soon knew every trail, and almost every herb bed, scaley bark and chestnut grove, and wild grape arbor for five miles around.

Johnny's female bull terrier that we had bred to Professor Gray's champion pointer Dash delivered three fine pups. His mother refused to let him keep only one of them —I had to keep them all.

We never dreamed of what hunting dogs this cross breed would make. Jack Prince trimmed their ears, and they looked like small mastiffs. By hard and patient training for two years we made them into the finest coon, wild hog and bird dogs in the mountains.

This was the year 1908. We hunted with small bows and arrows, using unberallow staves for arrows. It was most effective up to forty feet and accurate. We both could place an arrow in a six inch circle at that distance.

That year I collected only nuts, berries, herbs, grapes, flowers and muscadines. We killed some rabbits and three groundhogs.

Down under Green's View I had an experience killing a groundhog that stayed with me, and it came before me ten years later during a most perilous moment in my life.

At Gorman, Texas, I was pursued to be mobbed. I was hemmed in like that groundhog. I had no choice except to die fighting. To surrender would be certain death. If I killed the sheriff, I would die also. All I could do was pray for God's help.

That cornered groundhog came so vivid before me, and I heard the words: "He will walk away. Be brave. Be patient. You won't be harmed." The sheriff did walk away —at that moment. I have no explanation for this experience.

Johnny was a Christian boy. We had a lot in common, and he added a lot of happiness in my life.

My bodyguard business grew until I was employed two nights a week escorting the ladies to different houses, and waiting until the bridge parties was over. For almost two years I was busy with my mountain collections and waiting on my white people. I rarely had anything to do with colored people—except at Sunday school.

At that time we were blessed to have the fine Father sent to us named Stoney. He had a friend name Ambruster. Those two men gave much time to training our young boys to be good atheletes.

154

Father Stoney liked me very much, understood much of my troubles, and often talked to me. He encouraged me to take care of my Mama, and he tried to get me to go to St. Mary's school. He and Ambruster coached our two teams of football and baseball. We had the best teams of colored in the South.

At that time we had all kinds of entertainments—cake walks, minstrels, concerts. Fiske University, and the Meharry teams were invited to come and play with us. The whole town would turn out to see us play.

The summer of 1908 Ann came back to Sewanee on a visit.

She bought a goat and wagon from some tourist. The wagon was an exact copy of the Tennessee Wagon Co. wagons. She gave it to me so I could rent it out to the children at twenty five cents an hour. This would earn a dollar a day. I was in business.

I worked Billy for two seasons, and made many friends among the tourists. Billy and I had our pictures take many times every day. Our pictures went to every city in the South.

After the summer seasons I done a wood yard business —cutting stove wood and selling it to the colored people at twenty cents a load. I also hauled clothes and spring water for the white people. I met many fine people and some of them wanted me to go away with them.

In the fall of 1909 I had been confronted with two experiences that left memories hard to forget.

At the hotel one morning a tall blond man came to me and told me he wanted me to ride his daughter every morning for a month. His name was Fletcher, and he was from

155

Ohio. His daughter Nancy was the sweetest child I had served. He and his wife both were so kind. After a couple of weeks he paid fifty cents each day.

One morning he ask me a lot of questions about who my father was. I refused to answer. That day he gave me a dollar. He ask would I come Sunday morning and ride Nancy? I agreed.

I always shined shoes on Sunday morning. While I was waiting in front of the hotel Mr. Fletcher came out on the veranda and said: "You will have to wait a while for Nancy." He saw I had my shine box, and said: "You can shine my shoes while you are waiting." I shined his shoes, and he went back in the hotel.

While I was putting the polish back in the box one of the bellhops named Aldren came up to me cursing: "You have no right to hustle shines here in this hotel." He kicked me so hard I tumbled down the steps onto the sidewalk. I wasn't able to get up on my feet. He threw my shine box down.

Just then Mr. Fletcher came out of the hotel. When he saw I was hurt he ask me: "Didn't that nigger kick you down those steps? Tell me the truth—you are hurt. I'll kick him all over the hotel." I said: "No, I fell down the steps." He said: "Please tell me the truth. I saw him throw your shine box down. You are telling a white lie." I had learned that a Negro didn't have a chance at fighting a white man in the South, so I refused to tell the truth.

I was so crippled I had to go home. All I hoped for was that when I was big enough I would beat Aldren up myself.

Next morning Mr. Fletcher came to me, and said: "I

156

want you to take me to your foster mother. I knew you are an orphan. Bishop Gailor is your Godfather. I want to adopt you and take you to Cleveland with me. I want to give you a chance and an education. You are a fine boy —too fine to be here where you don't have chance." I said: "No, I have to take care of Mama. She needs me." He said: "I want to talk to her. Come, we will go to see her now."

He ask Mama if she would let me go to Cleveland with him. He would adopt me and train me to be a fine servant of the educated class. I would be sent to school, an Episcopal school, where I would receive training like young men of the white race.

He said: "The boy is a Christian. My wife and daughter are most fond him. He needs a chance. He will make a fine man. I will give him the best education that can be given. I have permission from both of his counselmen and his family on the white side. You are the only other one who must give consent."

He said: "Mattie, you have done a fine job teaching him to be a Christian and to work. I learn he is resentful of many things that the colored people call him. He wants to go to school. If he was away from here he would soon forget these insults. If you will let me take him I will compensate you, as I know he helps you very much. We just like the boy. There are many people that want to help him. Will you let him go with me? I am secure financially."

Mama burst out crying, holding her apron up to her eyes: "It's like giving away my own. I've learned to love him like my own. I just can't say yes. I promised his mother as she was dying that I would do my best. If he wants to go I won't stand in his way." She turned her back.

157

I hadn't ever seen Mama cry like this. Suddenly, I realized she loved me. I went to her bent over the ironing board crying as if her heart was breaking. I told her I couldn't ever leave her. She soon gained control of herself, and said: "Mr. Fletcher, give us time to think it over." He smiled, and said: "I understand."

He said to me: "Are you going back to the hotel with me?" We left. On the way he ask me was the colored people here good to me? I didn't lie this time. I said: "Some of them. I love them." He said: "I know that. Yesterday you told a white lie to protect that dirty skunk that kicked you. Anybody that would harm an innocent boy like you needs to be punished. You are just loyal. I like loyalty. That's why I want to help you. You must go to school."

At the hotel Mrs. Fletcher and Nancy were waiting on the veranda. She ask quickly was I going home with them? Mr. Fletcher shook his head no. That was the last of that. They kept me around until time for Nancy to take her nap. They taken many pictures of Billy, Nancy and I.

When they told me good-bye he gave me a five dollar bill, and told me to always be a Christian and obey Father's advice. I never saw those wonderful people again.

That month had been profitable for me. I made over thirty dollars. From the ten dollars Mr. Fletcher had given me we were able to pay all of our due bills from the panic year of 1907. Mama and I counted the money we had left after all bills were paid. We had almost twenty dollars which put us in good shape for the winter.

Two days later I went to the hotel with Billy. There were no children to ride. Everybody was leaving because vacation was over.

As I started home I met a blond lady with a boy and a girl. The little girl ran to me asking could she pat the goat? She caught me by the hand, laughing and holding to my hand, saying: "I like you." Then the boy came to me. It seemed they wanted to be close to me. I ask would they like to take a ride? The girl ask me to hold her in my arms so she could pat the goat on his back.

The lady stood a distance from us, just looking. I hadn't seen her for several years. Once, in a toy store, she told the owner to let me have anything I wanted, and charge it to her. I had asked the storekeeper who she was, but he didn't tell me.

I put the children in the wagon. The lady said: "Don't go very far. I will wait here." On our return, the girl did not want to get out. When I attempted to lift her she clung to me, saying: "I don't want to go." The lady came to us: "Ely has to go home, so let him go." The girl still held on. This seemed to vex the lady.

She came towards us and told the girl to turn me loose. I was laughing. She put her hand in my hair, and clenching my hair with a shake, said: "It's a pity you are so close, and not." Yanking the child out of the wagon she tossed me a half dollar, and said: "Get going." I went on my way wondering what was wrong that I had done.

I stopped at the Supply Store leaving Billy tied. When I came out Sam Bell had taken Billy for a ride making him run by pulling his tail. He ran him up and down the street until he was winded and went to his knees. I was angry, and crying. Sam called himself having a good time.

Henry Hoskin was the only person that told Sam he ought to be ashamed of himself. As small as I was I wanted to fight with Sam. He kept me away from him with his buggy whip. It was an hour before Billy could start home. This was the last day of my goat service.

When I got home I told Mama about the lady saying it was a pity that I was so near and not, and how she clenched me in my hair, and how lovably the children were and the woman so different it seemed she hated me. Mama kept ironing and didn't answer me.

I ask her: "What could be wrong that she didn't like me? All white people like me, Mama." She turned to me looking most serious, and said: "My son, you didn't know that was your Auntie and those were your brother and sister you were riding. She meant that you were so near white and not."

I said: "Mama, I will find some other way to make money. I won't be no servant for my brother and sister. I won't be their nigger." This was the first time Mama didn't scold me for refusing to be a nigger. I told her how Sam had misused Billy. "I am going to protect everything I own from now on if I have to die trying. I'll get even with Sam when I am older."

She said: "No, don't think of fighting with white people. A Negro just don't have any chance. I don't want you to have that in your mind. Jack Prince was here today. He wants you to go and see Ned. He said Ned is in a bad way and is losing a lot of his hogs and cows by not keeping sober enough to milk and feed them. Since his wife has left him he has been going down."

I reminded her that I would be sixteen years old in two weeks. I would be ready for a gun. She said: "Not if

160

you talk about fighting. The shot gun that Aunt Charlotte gave you is yours on your birthday." I was so happy that she had consented.

I went to see Johnny McKay and we had a long talk. He was glad I didn't go to Cleveland. We made plans how we would rove the mountains that fall.

We spotted every tree from Roark Cove to Tick Bush where chestnuts, scaley barks, walnuts and grapes grew. By December I had sold twenty five dollars worth of nuts to the school boys. Many times I traded nuts to the students for clothes which I sold to colored people. It was all business. I was also busy doing bodyguard two nights a week, selling candy on Saturday afternoons, cutting wood for my twelve custermers, and delivering what washing Mama could do.

When school was out for the winter I had no income except wood selling, and I spent much time with Grandpa trying to stop him from drinking. I soon found that my being around him helped him a lot. He straitened up a bit for the next six months.

Jack Prince ask me to come and help his son Henry hew cross ties at fifty cents a day. He also let me have a thirty-two Winchester rifle for five dollars which I could pay at fifty cents a week. I didn't like that muzzle-loading shotgun at all. When it was raining sometimes it wouldn't explode.

Every day for three months for an hour Jack and I would practice shooting and he would instruct me how to shoot. I was shooting jam up with him at the end. We were cutting cord board at forty feet away. He was most proud of my ability, and often said I would be the best rifleman the mountains had seen. In the next few years he tried to keep me around him all he could.

One afternoon, coming home from a hunt, I heard the Dakin's dog barking at the end of the graveyard and pigs squealing. This happened next to the corporation fence. I went to see if it was our pigs, but instead they were Jack Prince's. Henry Prince rushed up, snatched my rifle from me, and killed Constable Dakin's dog. The dog was supposed to keep hogs out of the corporation, and he had killed two of Prince's pigs.

Two weeks later I was subpenaed to court to witness in Jack Prince's behalf. I was asked to lie by swearing that Dakin's dog bit Henry. Dakin was suing them for killing his dog. I was pressured by the Prince family that if I was their friend I would swear in their behalf, and I felt I should do anything for them.

This didn't bother me until I was called to witness. The judge ordered me to put one hand on the Bible and repeat: "I swear to tell the truth, all the truth, so help me God." I could not answer him. Mrs. Prince rushed up, and said: "Say, yes." The Judge ask: "Did you see Henry Prince shoot the dog and the dog bite Henry?" I just couldn't speak. I bowed my head. He said: "To your seat."

I went out of the courthouse to the yard, very hurt to think I had lied to God. My lie won the case for them, and I eluded the Prince family for two months.

When Grandpa tried to suicide by taking rat poison my little brother found him not too late, and the doctor saved him. Jack heard about it, and came to the house. He called me aside: "The old polecat has suffered a lot. That's

162

why I told you to stick close to him. You know he is a fine man. He is one of my best friends." Then, he said: "Red Horse, my door is always open to you. If the worst should happen you have me to come to anytime." These words touched me deeply, and I forgot all about the resentment I had held against the Princes.

I went home with Jack and had supper with his family. This led me to the greatest friendship of a poor white family I ever had. They were so democratic that I never felt like a nigger or a bastard when I was around them. He ask me would I help him do some castrating of pigs? I could hold them while he operated on them. I was glad he asked me to help as I wanted to learn as much of vetinerian work as I could.

I went back to Grandpa's house to find he was resting easy. A friend of his would feed and milk the three cows. My Aunt Ada had come to care for him. He snapped out of his regrets in the next few days, and lived almost two years before he died a natural death. I spent many nights with him.

There wasn't much happiness for me at that time— just to sell small bits of salt rising and beaten biscuts for Mama to a few people left in town.

There was a colored man name Jim Jones, a cook at St. Luke's building, who repaired clocks in his spare time. He was much different from the other colored people. He never taken part in no amusement, and was always busy. He liked me. He advised me to learn a trade, and suggested I should learn to repair shoes so as to have something to do at all times.

I went into the village to the shoe shop, asking the

owner could I stay around and watch him work? I would keep the shop cleaned up. After ten days I bought a last and half-soled two pair of my own shoes which I exhibited, cutting the price to where I could profit fifteen cents a pair of shoes. This caused me to make five dollars that winter.

The spring of 1909 was the most wonderful, I believe, in the history of the Rome of the South, Sewanee. We came forward with championship material, both football and baseball. We servants champt over all colored teams. S.M.A. also came forward with fine atheletes—such as Jinx Gillem, Captain Gillem's son. He and Jack Sneed were the spark plugs of the S.M.A. team that trounced all professional schools of the South.

The Varsity had been presented with such great atheletes as Lex Stone, Faulkenberry, Sike Williams, Eric Cheap, Aubery Lanier, Mac Milliam, Johnny Greer, and their spark plugs Chigger Brown, Ward, and Fox. Over three years I believe all of the men received all-Southern honors. I, too, as a mascot, because they let me wear a white sweater with a purple S on it. Chigger Brown, my idol, gave it to me.

I hustled the bat for baseball, and carried the bucket of water with oatmeal on a sponge at football. Once they taken me with Six, the trainer, to Nashville. I learned to massage arms and feet, and to make linement of birch oil and witch hazel. This helped me to aid Mama with her rhumatism, and I didn't have to buy much Sloan's linement anymore.

That year I gained another friend—Happy Gillem, Jinx Gillem's younger brother. He donated me all of his off-cast clothes, and I became to be the best dressed colored boy in town. I still had my troubles with the poor white trash, and the dislike of some of the Negroes. I was now growing up big as the ones older than I. Mountain exercise was developing me rapidly.

I was keeping customers supplied with clebric water, flowers, berries, and paupau apples. Jack taught me how to de-fang a rattlesnake for a month, so it would be harmless. If I couldn't catch them without risk, I would kill and skin them and tan the skin to make vestfronts or belts which the students would buy.

Rattlesnakes over thirty inches the circus would buy at two dollars a piece. My dogs became to track the rattlers. This cause me to kill many of them. I had two cigar boxes of rattlers when I left home. Many students sported vests of rattlesnake skin.

Fathers Stoney and Armbruster was spending a lot of time with the colored people, teaching us to be atheletes and coaching our teams. Their favorites were Yum Yum, and Simon and Houston Smith. Those boys was real big league material. I wasn't developed to compete with them, so I concentrated on boxing.

In the fall of 1910 Father Tyson, who presided over St. Augustus, sent for me. He told me he was buying a pack of hounds from the Miss Kennels. They were English hounds. He wanted me to be his hunting guide and trainer for the dogs.

He explained to me that I could start my own kennel for breeding. He would give me a pair of thoroughbreds. I had already begun raising fox terriers that people came to buy from as far away as Nashville. I taken up his offer.

Father Tyson had a colored butler named Zemma Hill who was training to be a minister of the Baptist faith. He became to be the pastor of the Edge Field Baptist Church of Nashville, Tennessee, where he remained at least thirty years as one of the most reputated ministers of the Negro race in the South.

Zem and I would run and drag a coonskin through the woods and Father and the dogs would follow up the trail. This experience caused me to forget every other method of making money. I had found what I wanted to be in the mountains.

Father taught me to make carbide lamps. We manifactured our own as there were no flashlights. We only used the lamps when we had treed an animal. With the lens of a magnifying glass the lamps were good for twenty five yards, and we could search a tall tree easily.

For two months we didn't see a coon. Paying up to five dollars I had bought every dog that I was told could tree a coon. Grandpa's dogs had been stolen or had died, and there just wasn't no coon dogs left in town.

That was a year of many changes. I began to feel like I was a man. Houston Smith had taken up my body-guard work as I didn't want that work any more. I concentrated on work with the atheletes, and on the mountains— hunting, trying to learn to be a barber, and shoe repairing.

Father Tyson had equipped a work-shop for his two oldest boys. He had bought three horses for them. I could use one anytime I wanted. He had eleven children, and I was told he was a wealthy man. He was very fond of me, and like to take walks when I was around. He gave me a compass, and taught me to read the stars—such as the dip-per. The only other guide I had some foggy nights in the mountains was the Breslin Tower Chimes which could be heard in the canyons as far away as four miles in the still of the night.

Father explained to me that the fur business was being operated and I could sell all kinds of skins. He wrote to St. Louis to the fur commissioners and secured a price list. This started me to trapping and hunting every minute during the season, and for the next two years the mountains was my home.

I first attempted to buy furs from the mountaineers, but not knowing what I was doing I got stuck on my first deal, and had to lose fifteen dollars on a twenty five dollar deal. I bought those skins on credit and discovered they were too old. I tried to explain that the skins were too old, showing them the report, but it made no difference to the mountaineers. I had made a bargain, and I had to pay them when I got the money. I knew I had to have their friendship if I expected to fare well in the mountains, so I kept my bargain.

One afternoon near Shakerag hollow I heard pigs squealing. I dismounted and sneaked around the shoulder of the canyon thinking there was a fox taunting the pigs. It was old Man Wat Cannon who Grandpa had called a hog rustler. He had found the sow and six pigs and had bayed the sow by feeding her corn. He was marking the pigs with his mark.

The sow had belonged to Grandpa. I was within forty feet of him before he saw me. I yelled at him asking why was he marking our pigs? He stood looking at me for a moment, then ask: "Are you old Ned's grandson?" I said:

"Yes." He was an old man with whiskers almost to his belt. He laughed: "Son, you know my eyes are failing. I was sure that sow had my mark on her." I had heard that whenever he was caught in this act this was his excuse.

Then, he said: "I have heard that you are pretty damn cocky to be a nigger. You had better drop a buttonhole lower if you expect to rove these mountains." He got on his old gray mare and started to ride away, but then he saw my two dogs that was yoked together.

He came back to me, asking: where did I get those dogs? He said: "I will give you twenty dollars for them. Those are the finest dogs I ever saw." I said: "They are not for sale. I am going to make coon dogs out of them. Do you know anybody that has a good coon dog that I can buy?"

He got off his horse and went to the dogs, examined them, then said: "I got to have this male dog. I tell you what I will do—I will trade you the smartest coon dog in Tennessee and give five dollars to boot for that dog. See that shepherd dog there? He is the best coon dog in these mountains. I am getting too old to hunt at night. If he don't do what I say he will you bring him back to me, and I will give your dog back and you can keep the five dollars. This will make up for my mistake with the pigs."

It was hard to give up Heck as the two dogs were so beautiful as a team, but I wanted the old man's friendship. I agreed. That was the best trade I ever made. The old man and I became to be close friends. He gave me many advises of where good hunting was found.

The shepherd dog was eight years old. He had caught so many wild hogs all his teeth was gone except his four tusks. He had gashes all over his body from cuts by wild hogs.

I went straight to Father Tyson and told him about my new dog. He went hunting that night. Shep treed two coons which inspired us and our dogs.

That was the beginning of the finest pack of hunting dogs I have ever heard of. Wild hogs, squirrels, possums, coons—we never lost not one trail for the rest of the time we hunted. Shep treed over three hundred dollars worth of fur in the next two years. We often had hunting parties of men who just wanted to see our dogs work. Father Tyson hunted just one night a week. Other nights I had to hunt alone. No colored people wanted to hunt. Johnny's mother didn't want him out after nine oclock.

Having a fine tree dog was the answer to all my prayers. The mountains was my home—the Negroes and the white trash could have the town, just so long as they didn't bother me. Every way things changed. Mama began to be closer. I was almost her full suport because her son that wasn't married was coming down with poor health. The two or three dollar a week I made kept us eating.

I must tell a ghost story.

I was discouraged by—or attempted to be—by many of the Negroes who said I would be found dead in the mountains. I was told of two places where ghosts had run hunters away. I accepted these reports as a joke after Father Stoney told me there was no such thing as a haunt. He said people who supported fear might believe anything, and he told me—the first time I heard it—the phrase "Fear is man's worst enemy."

One night I started to go down the mountain and came

upon a trail as I passed the Palmer home. I thought of one of the ghost stories I had heard.

There had been a lady name Nancy Bannon. She had been a victim of a fire, and was found in the ruins of her house. Everybody pondered over this as a mystery that she didn't escape the fire. About the same time some fox hunters' dogs struck a trail just pass the Palmer home that led to a hickory tree on a hill, four hundred yards away. The dogs acted so mysterious—leaping in the air, snapping at the air—that the men ran away, claiming it was a ghost. They claimed they heard a woman screaming up that tree. No one hunted in that area because of this rumor.

A hundred yards past the Palmer home my dogs struck a hot trail that caused them to bay at the lone tree on top of the hill. When I got to the tree the dogs were so excited they were gnawing the bark on the trunk of the tree. I was sure we had a coon. Soon I could see there was nothing.

The moon was high and bright. I could see everything to the top of the tree, and it was a tall one. It wasn't close to any other trees. Just then the ghost story came to my mind. I decided I would climb the tree to prove to the dogs that they had lied. The same performance I had heard of began—the dogs leaped in the air, snapping at something, running to the woods, yelping like they saw something above them. I could feel cold chills down my back. I knew I was seeking something I couldn't find.

While I was trying to find the answer, they came rushing back up to the tree on a hot trail and bayed again. I was too puzzled. I decided I would climb the tree. I knew that nothing had come by me. At that moment the dogs began leaping in the air and racing down the hill yelping. I decided: "If I have stay here all night, I am going know what this is."

I would build a fire on the dark side of the tree. I gathered some dead wood. As I was stacking it beside the tree, I heard the dogs coming toward me on another hot trail. Just then I felt something run up my leg to the top of my head and leap off it to the tree. I just glimpsed it going up the tree, and thought it was a mouse.

The dogs crashed against me, leaping up the side of the tree. As I backed away, I saw Shep was standing twenty feet from the tree, as if waiting like he did for a coon to jump from the tree. He knew their habits and planned to intercept it. Suddenly, the dogs acted up as before and ran down the hill—all except Shep.

I saw he was shaking something he was holding in his mouth. I made him drop it, and found it was a flying squirrel.

It turned out they had a den in the hollow of the tree, and would race up the hill on foot, climb the tree, leap off of it, and glide down to other trees. Shep had solved the problem and caught one as he opened his wings to glide. Mr. Judd had told me the flying squirrel was kin to the bat, and belonged to the mice family. Now I knew the ghost story was a hoax. As soon as I let each dog smell the squirrel they were under control again, and we went on with our hunt.

Next morning I told the story and displayed the squirrel at the barber shop of Hugh Hills. Professor Norton, General Calmore, and Mr. Judd was there getting their grooming done. I was congratulated by the notables for being brave enough to weather the experience I had and for solving the mystery. This became to be town gossip. I was sure that I had nothing more to fear in the mountains.

Next afternoon I was going to the village to buy cartridges, and saw Grandpa on a bender. He was arguing with two younger men in front of Pink's Pool hall. He was well loaded. When he was in this condition, he could be very nasty.

The other men didn't know I was his grandson as they hadn't been living in Sewanee very long. One of them decided he would give Grandpa a beating, and started to hit him with a broken cue stick. I walk up back of Grandpa. He hadn't seen me. He had been abusing the men.

One man struck at the old man barely missing his head, and Grandpa staggered back. I rushed toward them with my rifle pointed at the man, telling him if he hit Grandpa I would kill him. They retreated. Getting Grandpa in a sulky, I carried him home. He boasted as usual all the way home of what a terror he had been, and how many men he had killed in his time. He said that I was a chip off the old block, and would be just like him.

After getting him in the house, I unhitched the horse, looking around to see how things had diminished around him. Only a few chickens and hogs remained, and the old horse was underfed, looking like death knawing on a cracker. I became to feel the hurt or regrets Grandpa was carrying, as soured as he was.

He asked me to stay a while with him. After drinking two cups of his strong coffee he sobered up a bit, and began telling me about his troubles, and how people had deceived and robbed him, and how they had broken up his family. I would have to help protect him. I was all he had. "Don't let nobody take nothing from you. Make people respect you like you did today."

It seemed he had lost interest in everything. Revenge was all he was thinking of. Now and then he would make boasts about how tough he had been, and me knowing he hadn't ever hurt anyone in his life—except himself.

I ask: "Why don't you pray, Grandpa? God will help you." He said: "I just can't get it. I don't say there is not a God, but I don't get this Resurrection. Father Eastern and Father Clabern talks to me. I just can't get it. I know you are a Christian. You have to be the way these niggers have treated you because a white man is your daddy. And it's not your fault. Don't let them kick you around anymore, Christian or no Christian. I want you to be a man among men like me. Don't have no boss. Make your own job."

Then, he said: "You and Trudy are the best looking nigger boy and gal in Sewanee. You get closer to her. Don't let no dude nigger pull her down. She is the prettiest white gal in Sewanee, even if she do have to be called a nigger. Your Aunt Ada is going to need help. I don't go about her. I don't like that husband of hers. I will shoot him if I catch him beating her. You do it, too. He is just mean and a bully. Don't let him bully you around. Remember this—don't talk about nothing that you hear from the mountaineers. They all like old Ned because I don't talk. You will get along well in the mountains."

This was the first time Grandpa had let me talk back to him. He ask me to bring him a possum every week. It was four o'clock when I said I must be going. He was pushing the embers off the dutch oven where he had a big possum and sweet potatoes for his dinner.

Then, he said: "I want you to remember this—there is a cave a little ways from Poplar Springs. It was filled up by the Indians years ago. There is a treasure hid there—my spirits has told me. There is a hole in the ground. It take a rock some time to hit bottom. You are big enough to go down in it. We will do that when Spring comes." He said: "Wat Cannon stopped by two days ago, and told me about you trying to stop him from marking my pigs. He claimed he thought they were his. I know he was lying. But the old hog hustler ain't too bad. He is a friend to the nigger. His family had a plantation over in the Sherwood Valley, and he and two other brothers stands by their ex-slaves. You will hear some hellfire stories about how they have defended one of their niggers."

Grandpa added: "Whatever you hear about Alf Cannon, don't talk it to no niggers. Wat told me he traded you a good coon dog. He said he tried to bluff you, but you told him you had a right to protect your Grandpa's property. He said he like you. You are willing to give and take, and that's why he traded you his dog. He means right. He and Jack Prince are the best friends you can have."

I left him carrying all of his regrets on my shoulder. This was the first and last talk we ever had man-to-man. A few weeks later Grandpa died suddenly.

174

CHAPTER
11

After Grandpa's burial there were many bills to be paid. I assumed all debts which would come to fourteen dollars. I would pay in time. This kept his farm from mortgage.

I would have to pay some way. Studying my fur list I found that skunks was the highest-priced fur around—as much as two fifty a piece. I killed and skinned everything that had hair on it except dogs. Housecats went with everything else. I wasn't allowed to stay in the house when I had caught skunks at night. I would sleep in the barn with the dogs. As cold as it was we huddled together and slept warm.

I found two caves in the mountains where I bedded leaves and stocked wood. Here the dogs and I would stay many nights. By February the tenth I had trapped and caught one hundred and seventy pieces of skins.

I shipped them to F. C. Taylor Company, hoping I would get back enough to pay my bills. The check came and I couldn't believe it was true—the amount. I went to Mr. Brooks who ran the big grocery store with his two sons Bert and Preston. They were so kind to we colored people. I ask him to tell me how much was this check? As he looked at the check, he said: "Jimminy Christmas, where did you get a check for this amount of money?

Mat won't have to worry about her bills. What did you do to get this amount of money? This is eighty-seven dollars and seventy-two cents."

I ask: "Will you cash it and take out what Mama owe you?" He said: "I don't have that kind of money here. You take it to the bank tomorrow." Money was still scarce from the scrip years of 1907 and 1908. I went to Mama and showed her the check. From this time on it seemed that the skunk odor was the most welcome around home. I didn't have to stay in the caves unless I just wanted to which I often done.

I paid all of my bills, and gave Mama twenty-five dollars to buy her a coat, a suit and high-top shoes. I gave her sick son ten dollars to buy medicine. This left me twenty dollars to buy ammunition and steel traps.

Over fifty pieces of skins were no good, such as rabbits, weasels, groundhogs. The coons and skunks paid off. I had six weeks more to hunt and would make every day and night count.

The next week I had the most narrow escape of all my experience in the mountains. I had drilled many honey holes for coons at the water fall under Morgan Steep which was also our swimming hole. There was a log with one end in the swimming hole. I had drilled a honey hole in the log on the end out of the water.

When I came around the edge of the cliff I didn't see the coon. He evidently slid down on the other side so I couldn't see him. After I had made my way around the edge to the top of the waterfall I looked back to see the tail of a coon hanging down at the end of the log. This meant I had to go back on the trail on the ledge of the waterfall.

I heard crashing and rumbling up the canyon, and a cracking of timber. I stopped and stood against the end of a big boulder. Soon I saw an avalanche of branches rolling down over the waterfall, and then a pillar of water fifteen feet high dropped over the fall with a churning motion, sending stones and logs in all directions.

Everything around me was vibrating. The water rose up twenty feet during the churning. I clung to the boulder as water raced around me waist-deep. The water rushed down the mountain as quickly as it came. I soon sensed the Hodson's Dam had broken. This was the first time I became to know God had his arms around me.

I stood by the boulder which I had sat on many times meditating my troubles, and where one time I had believed my mother had come from heaven and talked to me. To me seeing the coon tail had been a miracle as I couldn't have escaped the forty foot chasm had I not gone back towards the coon.

The coming summer we had a larger swimming hole. The log had been lifted out of our way. Many times I had dived off the log to get coins the students toss in to watch me dive and find them. I claimed this spot as my waterfall. Here I taken shower baths before other people had the accommodation.

The game became to be scarce in Roark Canyon and Greens View. I shipped all my skins the first of April, receiving sixty dollars.

I began loaning money on guns, watches, rings and stick-pins to men that gambled—ten cents on the dollar by the week. They all were paid first of the month. The most I loaned was three dollars on anything.

This was when I got a pistol. I liked a thirty-two

speed. I bought it from a piano player. I began to learn to fight with a pistol. I had read many detective stories of Nick Carter. I was going to be a mountain lawman some day, and I meant to be good.

I went to Jack Prince asking him to teach me to shoot a pistol like him. He used a forty-five, but my arms were too small for a gun that heavy. He had told me this before. He said if I would buy the ammunition he would teach me all I need to know. He liked to pratice anytime. I spent many hours with Jack praticing over the next eight months.

In the afternoons I went to the varsity team baseball where I would chase balls. There were several colored men that praticed with them. They would hire our pitcher to pitch to the training men. That spring was the last of the great teams I had seen Sewanee produce. That squad of men were the most humanitarian young men I have ever known.

Houston Smith and I learned all of our ball-playing experience from praticing as service from them. Sike Williams, the varsity pitcher, taught me to hurl. I done very well.

That year was Jinx Gillem's sophomore year with the varsity team, and as a pitcher he was a sensation. He had more speed than any pitcher they had seen in many years. He hadn't lost a game until Georgia University came to play the Sewanee tigers. Sike Williams won his game. Jinx was knocked out of the box. We had expected Gillem to shut Georgia out.

I was told by the colored trainer of Georgia that his team had hired four of the speediest colored pitchers in Georgia to pitch to their team so as to be good against Gillem. It paid off. This was the last game I saw of the real fast atheletes. Georgia won two to one.

During the series Chigger Brown stole four bases. He was for two years the greatest base stealer in the conference. The batting trio was Chigger Brown, lead-off man Aubrey Lanier, and Lex Stone clean-up. Lex Stone was called the Bambino. I knew the history that team had made would never be forgotten in Sewanee.

Everything boomed in Sewanee that year. There were more young ladies during commencement than ever. The turkey-trot step had just come out, and the students all danced to the tune of You Beautiful Doll. Trudy and I went to see all the fraternity dances so we could practice them.

That year the selected most handsome student was named King, first baseman on the S.M.A. team. This was the ladies' decision.

Many students remained in Sewanee during vacation. Their families came as tourists. The lodging problem became to be a bit acute. The hotel opened the first of June. Students from Fiske and Meharry Universities came to work with many help from the Side Batton Hotel of Nashville.

Mont Eagle was like Sewanee. Many tourists brought nurses, and one chaffeur came. He was the first Negro I had seen driving an automobile. His people were friends of the Hodson family. He told me that the sagers at Pelham had thrown rocks at him as he drove through. There were many automobiles came through town that year. George Quintard was the only student that owned a car. He let me ride with him any time I was going his direction. He liked me. One time he said he was going to take me with him when he left school.

I went to work for Mr. Calmore. Miss Dora Calmore, his daughter, said she was going to teach me to be an English butler. I worked three hours in the morning and some in the evening. Rev. Harry Calmore came that year with his family from Cuba to visit his father.

The teaching I received in that nine months I never forgot. It gave me some of the greatest opportunities years later in the outer world.

The only part of the job I objected to was pumping the vacuum while Miss Dora ran the nozzle. This I would have to do on Fridays. She encouraged me to be clean and immaculate. I bought nice clothes and dressed every day to go to work. For the first time I was really happy. It didn't pay like hunting and trapping. My salary was ten dollars a month. I also shined shoes and carried laundry for Mama who had all she could do. Some new colored families moved in to work.

I asked my cousin Trudy to go with me to the big dance that was taking place. The college girls and boys from Mont Eagle Hotel were coming to be with other college students. We both would be eighteen in September of that year. I bought her an organdy evening gown for seven dollars, and myself a blue coat, white pants, pump slippers, a purple tie and socks like the Sewanee students wore.

We were the youngest at the dance. When we finished the first dance many of the college boys came to me thinking Trudy was my sister, and wanting to meet her. We both were good dancers. The student boys became much excited over the beauty of Trudy.

180

I met all the girls and their chapperones. We were annexed to them for the rest of the summer. Nobody spoke about me being a bastard. Instead, we were called the best-looking girl and boy in Sewanee.

That was when dating started with me. All of the ladies was a year or two older than I, but it didn't make any difference with them—they wanted to date. I was kept date busy.

Trudy fell in love that summer and got married.

That same year Sewanee had two colored teams—a first nine and a second nine. The first nine was one of the best teams in Tennessee. Both whites and colored was proud of that team. The players have long been remembered: Noble Phillips, Yum Yum, Joe Arldredge, Bud Arldredge, Cul, Tommy Davis, Fred Bryant, John McFarland, Walter Wooden, Billy Childress, Scott Davis, Strike Arldredge, John Knuckles, Abb Arldredge. Six was the trainer and Hugh Hill managed.

All the men had been coached by varsity coaches, and they were realy professional ballplayers without a league name. When some of them became sick or couldn't travel, Hugh decided to replace them with reserves. He taken four boys that had worked and trained with the varsity team—Houston Smith, Simon Smith, Simp Bonner, and I.

I was a good fielder and showed promise as a pitcher. Simp was the same as I. Simon was a fine catcher, and Houston was a first baseman and top batter. We were all pretty good at bat.

On the fourth of July we taken our first trip to Pittsburgh, Tennessee, a cook-oven and steel foundry town. It was a sporty little burg—and a good laboring town like

Birmingham for colored people. They had one of the best ballclubs around. The white people was fond of that team.

In Pittsburgh was the first automobile race I ever saw. Three striped cars raced down the street for a mile. It was the only street over four blocks long. We could see them as they pass by, and afterwards it was ten minutes before we could see across the street for the dust.

That night they were having a prize fight. No Negroes were allowed to attend. I wanted to see a prize fight. A colored boy I had known at Bridgeport, Pete Hill, worked at a livery stable next to the building where the fight was to be. He told me we could climb on top of the stable and look through the window. It was a good fight. I decided that I was going to be a fighter. Jack Johnson had just beat Jim Jeffries for the championship. This was the only sport where a Negro could compete with a white man.

Coming back home, I had more to tell than anyone else.

Two weeks later we were invited to Fedville to play. I noticed there were many half-white Negroes, more of them than dark ones. I wondered if they were bastards. During the game, one of our men cleated their second baseman, and started a fight. The law rushed in to stop it. While we were listening to the advice of the law, four middle-aged white men pointed to some of their players and said: "They are our sons. If you hit them with a bat, we'll kill all you Sewanee niggers."

The game got underway but there was no way for us to win because the white people on the sidelines refereed the game—the umpire mostly waited for their decision. It was something for me to think about that I was Sewanee's only half-white bastard. I had to fight all alone. That was my last trip with the team. After that I played only when visiting teams came. But I didn't hold any hard feelings against the Fedville people for their way of wanting to win.

I remember that earlier, in 1908, when Fiske University came to play our team, and Sewanee was leading by one touchdown nearing the end of the last period, Fiske was driving for the goal and had a first down on the ten yard line. They stalled there. It was impossible to penetrate the human wall of Sewanee. I saw Grandpa, Henry Woods, Pink Sims, and some white students was helping back up Sewanee's line. When the gun sounded Fiske was still on the ten yard line. This is some of how the Negro played ball down South fifty odd years ago. No matter how it ended it was just a matter of sport, and no one held a grudge because nobody wanted to see their home town team lose. In every town white people supported the colored ball players.

By the first of September all the tourists had vacated and the hotels closed. The schools would open on the fifteenth. I had met many good looking girls that summer, and for a few days I felt a bit lonely, especially knowing how the stigma of bastardy hung over me. All fun ended.

For the next two months I had to be busy. Winter wood had to be gotten in and cut into stove wood to supply my customers—at least eight wagon loads. Henry Prince was to haul it for a dollar a load, if I cut and helped load. Joe Willis would help saw at fifty cents a day. This amount of wood would supply for four months.

I had planned to make that winter a big success.

I would start hunting and trapping in November, which left me two months to gather chestnuts, scaley barks, walnuts, wild grapes, muscadines, and herbs.

Chasing up and down mountains was a good training program for a boxer as I planned to be. Endurance was most important, I was advised. Fathers Stoney and Armbruster encouraged me. Father Stoney had become to be more of a counseler for me than Father Eastern. He advised me and encouraged me to become to be a boxer. He liked atheletics.

Nights I set pins at the bowling alley for three hours. Dr. Joe Selden had built the alley two years earlier, and his brother operated it.

In the first tourment Jack Sneed barely missed bowling a perfect game which would have awarded him a thousand dollars. As he tried for the tenth strike one pin reeled a bit and wouldn't fall. This was the highest record of bowling while I was in Sewanee. Jack Sneed never came close to his record again.

I always had a chance to work. My whole ambition was to be strong and able to defend myself. Fight seemed to be my middle name. The bitterness I had carried for years was ready to explode.

It seemed the day I became eighteen the world changed. September the eleventh, this being my birthday, I went to my Aunt Ada's, who had worked for Dr. Richerson every since my mother died. She lived on the estate like my mother had. Aunt Ada was alone when I arrived. I told her I was eighteen that day.

She kissed me on the forehead, and said: "Do you know, I have been waiting a long time for this day? You can have what Lena left with me when she died. No one know this except me. You are old enough to know how things were. After you were born, your father was kind to your mother. He gave her many things. He sent them to her by Aunt Henrietta Ferris who raised him as his old mama. She cooked for their family thirty years."

She ask: "Do you remember the rings that your mother wore when she was buried?" I said: "Yes." She said: "He sent them to her by Aunt Henrietta at the same time he sent what I have kept for you." She handed me a small chamos bag. There were a stickpin set with an engraved design of the Virgin Mary and the baby Christ, mounted in gold, a set of stud-buttons with cuff-links to match, all gold.

Aunt Ada explained: "He said you would be a Christian because your name was taken from the Bible. Lena ask me to see that her rings would be on her fingers when she was buried. I kept them when she was so sick. I put them on her the morning she was put in the coffin. They were valuable—a ruby, a diamond, and a horseshoe ring of emeralds. Giving you this completes my sister's request. Do take care of them."

I ask her: "Who is my father?" She said: "I don't know. Lena never told me. There were three sons in the family. Which one was your father I don't know for sure. Aunt Henrietta is the only one that do know. She was your mother's closest friend. She won't tell you until you are twenty-one."

Aunt Ada ask me to go up to the house to see Mother Richerson. As I walked in the parlor Mother was sitting by the window. I spoke: "Hello, Mother." She was my Godmother. She said: "My boy, I should spank you. It's been three years since you been to see me. Come closer." She held her spectacles by the handle, and said: "You are a handsome boy."

Dr. Richerson roused up from a nap he was having on the leather sofa. "Where in the hell did you come from, you damn little scrapper? I ought to take my cane and tan your damn red hide. You know you are the only son Mama and I have. Come here to me." I went, knowing he was going to tap me with his cane. After that he began kidding me about when I was small.

They both were almost blind. I stopped a while with them. They told me that Bishop Gailor wasn't pleased with me for not going to school. I left telling them that I woudn't stay away so long, and that was the last time I was to see my Godmother.

I went back to Aunt Ada's and found Uncle Doss, her husband, had come home from his job on the railroad drunk and was beating on Auntie. I had heard he done this. Grandpa had told me to shoot him if I caught him in the act. He was so busy slapping her around he didn't hear me come in. His pistol was lying on the table. I grabbed the gun and began snapping it at him. It wasn't loaded. I hit him on the head, knocking him down. I told him I would go and get my gun, and come back and kill him.

I ran home, got my gun, and started back. Aunt Ada had stopped Charlie Roe and Tommy Davis, telling them to stop me. This they done, taking my gun away. It seemed that Mama and all of the family was down on me.

Two days later, I beat up two boys that had picked on my little brother, and then their larger brothers beat me. I didn't have but four young colored boy friends in the town. Joe Willis was the best. He was helping me saw wood four days a week.

I was often taunted by the larger boys, saying I was just a bluff! I was like my Granddaddy—a big boast. I wasn't going to shoot nobody. This caused me to hope someone would do anything to me so I could have a cause to shoot him. I was hoping someone would call my bluff. It had to come. I was carrying my Grandfather's revenge as well as mine.

September the twenty-fifth Mama ask me to go and get Dr. Lear to come and see my foster brother, Scott. I hadn't ask Mama what his complaint was, though he had been ailing for a year. When the doctor was leaving he call me, and said: "Go and have this prescription filled. Tomorrow morning you come to the hospital. I want to talk to you."

Next day the doctor invited me to come in to his office and sit. "I have to talk with you because you are providing for Mat and her family. Your brother Scott is suffering with a very serious sickness in the second stage. He has a chance yet to be cured. Why didn't you tell Dr. Selden or me about it?" I said: "I didn't know of it."

Then, he said: "There is a new medicine produced in Germany. I haven't used it. I will have to send to the St. Louis laboratory to get it. The hospital don't furnish this type of treatment. You people will have to pay cash for it. Each shot will cost twenty-five dollars. We will have to have at least three—if not more. There will be other medicine, too. It will take six months to complete the course. How long will it take you to get seventy five dollars together? You don't have to worry about my fee—that can come anytime afterwards. All of the expenses won't be over a hundred and fifty dollars. This is his only chance to live. I don't want to start this treatment unless I am sure I can complete the course."

This seemed like a fortune to me when very few colored people earned over a hundred dollars a year. He said he could control the ailment for at least a month. "Don't talk to anybody about it. Mat don't want no one to know about it." I left him, saying: "I will let you know soon." I prayed all the way home.

I went to Mama and told her what the doctor had said. She said: "I don't know where to turn to get that much money. If you hadn't tried to be such a man and tried to shoot your Uncle Doss we might borrow some money from Ada. They work the year around." This hurt to hear it that way.

I told her I had twenty-two dollars. She didn't know I had any money. She got the jar she kept her money in. We counted over twenty dollars she had saved from her laundry work. She said: "I have been helping my son with medicine and paying doctor bills for a year, which is why I don't have any more." I told her that I had over twenty dollars owing to me for watches, rings and two pistols. "I can't collect any of it until the first of November, as the men has just started back to work."

Mama looked so worried. I hadn't ever seen her so let down. I said: "Give me the twenty dollars. I will get this treatment some way. I am going to make that hundred and fifty dollars in the next six months. I am going to borrow some money from Mr. Calmore." Mama said: "No, you will have to tell why you need it." I pledged that I wouldn't tell anyone. She gave me the money.

I pawned my rifle and jewelery to Hugh Hill for ten dollars. I taken fifty dollars to Dr. Lear the next morning asking him to start the treatment. I would have another twenty-five dollars by Thanksgiving. He smiled: "I know you will, Ely. I will send for the shots at once."

When I told Mama the deal I had made, for the first time she put her arms around me, and said: "You are the boy I hope you would be. We will get it paid some way. You are the arm of the family—I have to depend on you." This gave me a superior feeling that I was somebody. I don't know if it helped in one way—because of the bitterness I carried, I was still anxious to strike back at anyone that had mistreated me, and there was a lot of them, young and older.

At that time of season it was a bit dull for me. For the next three weeks I could collect nuts and herbs. I explained to Mama my plans: I would work at the bowling alley every night until hunting season. I would sell candy, crullers and peanuts for Mrs. Beasley every afternoon at ball practice, and shine shoes Sunday mornings. The only time I wanted free was to go to Sunday School and church.

I had learned that Negroes and sagers was much alike, looking for something for nothing. Each had taken from me because I was trying to buy their friendship. All that Grandpa had told me seem to come to thought— protect everything you have, keep your own money, don't be on your knees to nobody. Let people know you are a man.

I had no girl friend. The larger boys had shoved me

away when I tried to walk along with the girls. This I wouldn't let be no more. My gun would answer to what my fists couldn't do.

By the twentieth of September I had four cords of stove wood cut and racked. I let the people that had wood cooking stoves come and get their wood at twenty cents a load. Mama looked after this, as she was crippling badly, and couldn't stand on her feet to do washing. This paid two dollar a week until in January. Every penny we got was put in the jar at the head of Mama's bed. We charged everything of food at the grocery.

Dr. Selden agreed he would pay me half-a-dollar each night at the alley. He said I was quicker setting pins than the other boys. I know he wanted to help me.

I was still beating up boys that picked on my brother. I was beaten up by John Boyle on the first of October when I attempted to collect three dollars he had borrowed on his watch. He wanted to pay the three dollars without the one dollar interest he also owed. I refused to let him have the watch. He knocked me down, taken his watch and kicked me about. He was much larger and older than I. He also was a bully.

I went home and got my shotgun, as I didn't have my rifle, and went to look for him. He saw me first, and ran. I chased him, shooting at him. Many men tried to stop me. I turned towards them, threatening them not to interfere. I swore I would kill anyone that touch me. There were at least twenty of them. They just look at me as if I was crazy.

That night John sent me my money. Next day I told everyone that owed me that I meant to be paid. Everyone paid me. After that event very few people talked to me. No one tried to push me around.

Next Sunday at Sunday School Father Stoney gave me a severe lecture, alone, about my conduct.

After that I walked along with the girls, laughed and kidded with them, and all the older boys just looked on. It seemed the girls were amused at the stand I had taken. This started them to flirt with me.

They would slip out at night and date me in secrecy. It seemed they did not care to be in public with me. It seemed for the next six months that the young women and girls kept me busy dating—all in secret. I thought I was raising a fog, until March. I was much elated to think how I was getting back at the older boys.

By November the first I had stripped all of the gensand beds, taking every particle of roots. I did the same with quiene and other roots. I collected three pounds of gensand at seven dollars a pound and twenty pounds of other roots. I sold them all for thirty-two dollars in Winchester. This I paid to Dr. Lear.

I abused everything I collected from—sawed the limbs off the chestnut trees and the scaley barks.

I wanted every penny I could get and as quick as possible. Stripping the trees of every nut I could get, for twenty days I was in the mountains from six to eight hours a day—except Sundays and Saturdays. The only money I spent was to buy cartridges for my pistol. I practiced with it every day.

My dogs got exercise and training, too. That was when I trained the two husk-mouthed dogs to be my body-gaurds. They would let me know when we were approaching either man or animal a hundred yards away.

That year I collected black walnuts—ten sacks. Will Ray let me dump the walnuts in his cow pen. The cows with their split hooves cleaned the hulls off. Then, I put the walnuts on top of the house to let the rain wash them and the sun season them. I made over twenty dollars from nuts, grapes and muscadines.

The first of November Mama and I counted our money in the jar—it was all in silver. We had thirty dollars. I taken ten dollars and got my rifle out of pawn. Mama was most happy her son had begun to respond to the treatments.

My own trouble hadn't lessened any. I was being threatened by some of the colored men about dating their women and girls. I also had to fight with some of the sagers.

One afternoon in the village there were some Tick Bush sagers. One was the one who had broken my collarbone three years before. There were nine of them in all. They attacked me in front of Mr. Rosborough's store. They must have thought I was going to run like most of the colored boys. I picked up a stick and started to flail them with it.

Mr. Rosborough and Father Armbruster came out of the store with Mr. Sam Winn and stopped the fight. All the sagers quieted except the older Newby boy. He told them he didn't like this nigger—meaning me—and he was going to beat hell out him and it wasn't any of their business. I hadn't heard a sager talk to no aristocrat like that before.

Father Armbruster said to me: "Do you want to fight him?" I said: "Yes, sir. Just keep the others back." He had trained me to box himself. He said to Mr. Rosborough and Mr. Winn: "Let them fight. Ely can whip all of them, one at a time."

The fight was on. It didn't take long before Newby

192

was bleeding from his mouth and nose, and one of his eyes was closed. Then his smaller brother taken it up. He was exactly my size. He was down on the ground quickly. Mr. Winn told them to get out of town, and not bother any more colored people.

This caused the sagers to attempt revenge. The next Friday night was a dance at the Odd Fellows' hall. The Tick Bush sagers came in the dark close to a hundred yards with rifles and shot at the dance hall. No one was injured. Many of the colored men had guns and returned the fire. The sagers got on their mules and raced out of town. That was the only conflict I have known to happen between colored and white people.

I knew it was not the end of my troubles. I was much alone. I was becoming more bitter day by day to both Negroes and poor white people.

Everything I had prayed for seemed to come out right. The first of November I dropped all work and went in to the mountains to trap and hunt. I soon felt like I was where I belong. I never felt alone in the mountains.

I had a fine pack of English hounds. Father Tyson had gone to New York for a while, and I had fallen heir to any of his dogs that I wanted to use. That pack of dogs became to be the finest combination of dogs I have heard of.

I worked them with this type of strategy: Two cold-nose pot-licker hounds would build up the trail. Then, the English hounds—faster than the cold-nose dogs—taken up the trail. When the trail was hot enough I would send the three husk-mouth dogs in. Two of them were crossed between pointer bird-dogs and bull terriers. The third was a shepherd.

193

Those husk-mouths were faster than English hounds. While Mr. Coon would be playing tricks topping trees, the husk-mouths would almost catch him on the ground. The husk-mouths could tree as much as a quarter of a mile ahead of any hound. That way we never lost a coon unless he made it to a cave. When day hunting the bird and bulldog cross dogs would point and retreave birds and tree squirrels. Put on a leash, they would track wild hogs.

As the season opened I found almost every mountaineer was trapping and hunting for fur. The news of how much I had made the previous year had caused these people to try hunting. I was confined to just two canyons—Roark and Green View. I trapped in one and hunted in the other. It didn't take long for my pack of dogs to clean up the game since we was hunting every night. I skinned everything that had hair from housecats to civet cats. By the first of December I had stripped the two canyons.

There wasn't but one other man that had good hunting dogs. His name was Mitchell. He and his two sons were friends of mine. He lived beyond Two-mile Branch. I decided I would go to Mitchell's and hunt with them one night leaving home about four o'clock in the afternoon. It was foggy and I had to go near three miles. I went over the railroad close to Tick Bush. By following the railroad I would avoid much of the wet foliage.

As I crossed a small tressel the dogs struck up a hot trail in the woods about five hundred yards away. There were headed toward me. I made ready to shoot whatever it was as it crossed the track. I was expecting it to be a fox. The tressel was very low, not more than four feet high. I knew there was a wet weather stream coming down this draw. The foliage was thick in the ravine.

194

As I was sitting on the tressel two turkies raced through the opening at the bottom of the tressel. There was no chance for a shot. The dogs came across the tracks with their noses in the air going to the mountainedge where the turkies glided away down the canyon. The dogs soon came back.

This took place at the site of the second ghost story I had heard about. I knew if I told what I saw I would be called a liar. Two days later I came back: the same performance started. I got down in the ditch. Mr. Gobbler and two hens came so fast I let both barrels of buckshot go, I got all three. Coming back on the track there was four of the Tick Bush loggers passing. I told them the way I discovered it was turkey. They resented my theory and still claimed the place was haunted. General Calmore got the gobbler, Mr. Judd got one hen, and Doc Barton got the other.

My traps began to be robbed, and some were stolen. My dogs treed a coon in Shakerag hollow one night. Four men came to me telling me their dogs had treed the coon and I should get away from there. Two of them had guns. I gave in to them, telling them not to try it again. I had a girl with me that had slipped out of her home just to be with me. That was why I didn't try to protect my own.

I went to Jack Prince, and told him about the loggers. He advised me to move my trapping to Tallys Fork where I would find more skunks on the southwest of the range than on the north. That was when I learned that some animals migrate to the afternoon sun—skunks, for an example.

December fifteenth I shipped my first shipment to F. C. Taylor Company—two hundred and ten second-grade pelts that had become to be well furred. My check was seventy-eight dollars.

I went at once to Dr. Lear. He said: "Scott is mending rapidly. You can take your time to pay the other fifty dollars." He added: "I think I will start chasing skunk. No body is making money like you."

He rubbed his nose, winked his eye at the nurse, and said: "When you come back leave your pet skunk in the mountain." I knew what he meant, and I beat it out laughing to myself, and feeling proud to know such a fine man. I thought of the night he came to Grandpa's house to arrange a certificate for us to ship the corpse to Winchester. He stood by the coffin, patting Grandpa on the cheek, and said: "He was a grand old scout."

I told Mama I wanted to use the money to buy furs from the loggers that was still trapping. She agreed. I told her I didn't want her to put her foot on the ground for the next three months, and she didn't. She could do only piece quilts, and the cooking.

Mr. Calmore ask me to come and help Miss Dora for two days—Christmas Day and Eve. I should be sure to get rid of my skunks. Christmas day was open house to the students. I had to soak my hands in coal oil and smoke them over smoking rags to get free of the skunk odor.

I brought all of my steel traps in for a week. Many had been stolen. Johnny McKay was on vacation, and he wanted to hunt two days. I spent the two days with him shooting quail, rabbits and squirrels. Those were the last days we hunted together. I didn't envy him anymore as I did when he became to be a cadet. I understood by then that a Negro was just to be of service. It was great to have aristocrats for your friends. I was lucky.

CHAPTER

12

I had more presents given me that Christmas than ever before. I had to go to almost every house of the aristocrats to collect presents.

Mr. Calmore gave me an army overcoat like the kind that General Grant wore—blue broadcloth with a cape —and also a leather cap with earmuffs. He said: "Merry Christmas, Ely. Major Butt and I have made you a General instead of a cadet. This is General Grant's coat. Put it on." It fitted perfect. He said: "You can sleep anywhere and be warm." This was the greatest present I feel I ever received. It served its purpose the next three months.

Aunt Ada sent for me to come see her. I knew her husband had been sick. I hadn't seen them for three months.

Uncle Doss was smiling at me, and said: "I am not mad with you. I don't blame you for trying to shoot me. Since I have been sick I see things much different now. I will never be like I once was. I am through drinking. This blood poisoning in my leg for two months has put me in bad shape. I need some money for medicine. I hear you are making money. You are a hustler. Mat is lucky to have a young man like you. I know you have a burden. I have a pistol I want to borrow ten dollars on until I get back to work. The doctor claims I will ready in a month. I don't get any treatment free like the people that works for the university."

He handed me a blue steel thirty-two-twenty colt. He said: "This is the latest gun made." I hadn't ever seen anything I wanted as much as that gun. It seemed to just fit my hands. I gave him ten dollars. He said: "I am your friend in every way. I don't blame you for not letting these Negroes kick you around. I am back of you what ever happens."

When I looked at Aunt Ada tears were running down her cheeks but she was smiling. She only said: "If Lena could see you now." I was so happy and full I wanted to get away. I said: "I will bring you a rabbit soon."

The gun was so fine I had to go and show it to Jack Prince at once. He had some of his old cronies visiting him. I was invited in. Mrs. Prince said: "Ely, you are in time to have some of my blackberry wine and gingerbread." The four men was telling jokes and experiences. I became to know they were lawmen—deputies like Jack. I sat and sipped the wine, waiting for a chance to tell Jack about the gun.

Suddenly, Jack came to his feet, and said: "Crocket, Sawer, Watkins—I have a little polecat here. He is the grandson of the grandest old polecat that ever lived in these mountains. I have been teaching him to shoot for four years. He don't know that he has graduated. I want you all to see who will be the finest rifleman and gunman ever been in these hills. Come out and see this boy shoot."

Then, he said to me: "I have been friends with these three men for twenty-five years. It was hell in these mountains with the fueding moonshiners. Revenue men didn't last long. When it was too touchy for them we four taken over. One them lives close to Sand mountain, another near Tracy City next to the head of Battle Creek."

We all went to the barn. On the side was a horizontal line four feet long, a perpendicular line that made a cross, and a circle eight inches in diameter. Jack said he was six month gauging the horizontal, putting the bullet within three inches above or below, and from thirty feet away on the pull. Then, he had made the cross and circle. He had mastered that in three months with speed.

"Watch," he told them. "Shoot," he said to me. I tried the new gun, placing five out of six shots in the circle to his counting. Jack said to them: "Can you beat that?" Crocket said: "I pity the one that faces him." Watkins said: "It is too bad he isn't a white man—he would make a hell of a lawman." "That's what he wants to be," Jack said: "He has read every magazine of Nick Carter for the last five years. I have a lot of fun with him. My boy and he are close pals." I said to Jack: "Keep my gun. I am going to Tallys Fork tomorrow. I'll stop by when I get back."

Mama was most happy when I told her that Uncle Doss and I had become to be friends again. While eating supper I told Mama what my next plans were. Scott was up and had supper with us. I could see Mama was most happy to have him on his feet.

She said to me: "Son, why don't you go to the concert tonight? You haven't gone out to anything for four months. They are going to have some swell doing tonight. I wish you would go, but don't have no fight. Don't pay no attention to what these niggers say. You are their betters."

I knew this would be my last chance for the next three

199

months. I dressed my best even though I did smell like a polecat.

Uncle Calvin Childress put on a concert twice a year. He was our organist at the chapel, and a born musician. He couldn't read a single note of music, and just played and directed by ear. Ten years earlier he had a band, the first band Sewanee had. He still had many of the instruments in his care, and had tried to build another band, but we boys just wasn't interested in music.

The schoolhouse was packed. There were many students attended from S.M.A., and also Father Stoney's friends from St. Luke.

I had heard that a young lady was visiting Sewanee from St. Charles, Kentucky, but I hadn't seen her. She was a vocalist, and she open the concert, singing My Country tis of thee. I thought she was the prettiest little brown doll I had seen. She had tons of personality, as she pranced across the stage asking the audience to sing with her. She insisted everybody sing, even the students, and they applauded her back.

She said: "I will sing to you, and to this gentleman," pointing to me, "my love song." I was sitting in the first row. She sang Sweet Nellie Blond, demonstrating her emotions to me as she sang. I had fallen in love for the first time.

The concert was a great success. Afterwards there was a dance. The students left, and we pushed the benches around the wall. There was the strangest orchestra I ever heard of: Houston and Simon Smith and Arlandus Rankin, playing auto-harps and blowing harmonicas held by braces on their shoulders; Uncle Calvin blowing the cornet; and his daughter beating the drums. This was Sewanee's music, and we danced by it.

The beautiful girl was stormed by all the men and older boys. I stood back, looking on. They were trying to get her to dance. I could see she was trying to go clear of them. She came to me, and ask: "Do you dance?" I said: "Yes." She said: "Please take me in your arms." We glided over the floor to the tune of a waltz. She ask would I escort her home? I promised I would.

The boys were saying: "He stinks like a polecat." She ask: "Why don't they like you?" Then, she said: "I know why—you are just darn goodlooking. I want you all to myself." She was doing the talking because I didn't know how to talk romance. She refused to dance with anyone else.

I now began to feel important. I went to the older people and girls asking them to have a treat on me. They sold ice cream and pop for five cents an order. I had forty dollars, half of it in one dollar bills. I held it in my hand to show I had money to do what I please. I knew this was more money than any of the young guys ever had. Everyone I ask accepted. I could see this put everybody to thinking: "The little bastard isn't so bad to have around."

My little sweetheart sensed the meaning quickly: she sang as we danced. She said: "We have stole the show. Let's go home. I want to be alone with you."

We talked, knowing we both were desperate in love with each other. We made our vows, thinking there was nothing to blot our happiness, only to find a few days later that our families protested our love affair. There had been a feud between the two families from far back. We decided we would carry on regardless. She said: "We will live in sin if we have to. I won't give you up for no one." We planned to meet in secret—as often as three times a week. She often slipped away and went hunting with me at night. This lasted for two months.

The day after the concert I went to Tallys Fork to look it over. I stood on Natural Bridge Rock looking over the large canyon, shaped like a two-pronged fork. Each cove was from two to three miles long. Around the rims it was ragged and cliffy. Down in the chasm were several hundred acres of canebrake.

I saw smoke from a cabin down at the base of mountain. I headed for it. I wanted to meet some of the mountaineers. I had heard that there were a Negro lived over there named Alf Cannon. I had seen him in the village. He was always with some sagers. No Negroes in Sewanee knew him. Grandpa had spoke of him once.

When I got to the cabin I saw two of the cutest little brown dolls, about my age. The house was a typical log house with a hall through the center. The girls stood looking at me, dressed just alike in gingham. I spoke: "Hello." They didn't speak. I ask if Alf Cannon lived there. They just stood and looked at me.

A woman appeared in the door dressed like the girls. She ask: "What do you want?" I ask: "Could I speak to Mr. Cannon?" She went back into the house. Out came Cannon: "What do you want with me?" I explained: "I am going to do some trapping. Can you tell me what game is in here?" He said: "Wildcats, coons and polecats."

I ask him if he would hunt with me some. He said: "No, I don't want no company. And don't come here bothering me and my family." He called his daughters in and shut his door. As I turned to leave, he opened the door and said: "If you see hogs in the canebrake don't go in.

202

They are wild." He slammed the door. This was the first and last talk I had with Alf Cannon.

I soon found there were lots of skunk dens, and they were big ones. There were also lots of fox and coon tracks, and hog tracks everywhere. Working through the canyons I got turned around in the canebrake, and came out on the opposite side. It was three miles back across the canyon.

As I looked around, I saw smoke three hundred yards away soaring over the trees. I knew some one lived there. I went to the house. There was a small white boy playing in the yard. A woman came to the door dressed like all of the mountain women in a motherhubbard dress. Her hair was dropping down her back.

She wanted to know what I wanted. I ask: "Is the man of the house at home" She said: "Nope. He will be here soon. Won't you come in?" I told her I was lost, and wanted to know if there was a way to Sewanee with out crossing the canyon. She said: "Wait until my husband comes. It won't be long. It's dinner time."

Someone drove up in an ox team. She said: "There comes my oldest son." He had a load of wood. The little boy had been jabbering away asking about my dogs. The boy driving the oxen was darker than I by two shades—he looked like an Indian.

The little white boy said to me: "That is my half brother. His name is Andy. His father is a black man who lives in the canyon." Andy said: "Hello." I said the same.

Mr. Atkins came riding in on a black mare. He said: "Hello." As he got off his horse, he asked: "Who are you?" I told him I was Ned Green's grandson. "I want to ask about what kind of game is here in the canyon as I am going to trap." The wife came to the door, saying: "Come in. Dinner is ready." He said: "Come with us to dinner. The old gal has backbones, tomatoes, cabbage sprouts, cracklin' bread, and blackberry cobler."

He said: "Any of old Ned's family is good with me. I know you must be hungry. It's a long walk back to Sewanee." We went in to the table. He was a good-looking man to be a mountaineer, a heavy black head of hair that came low on his forehead, and well-built with broad shoulders.

At the table Andy sat on one side by me. The blessing was like every man for himself. I was so shocked over the white woman having a nigger baby, and a white man raising him, I couldn't talk for thinking and trying to listen. Little John, the white boy, kept jabbering. No one talked except Mr. Atkins and John. Andy just sat, looking down at his plate. I knew he was like me: a man without a country.

I was satisfied to here Mr. Atkins say: "Andy is my adopted son. His father is name Alf Cannon, a black man who lives down the canyon. He is my closest neighbor." The wife only spoke when she ask if we would have more food. Atkins told me all about the canyon, and invited me to come and hunt with him and Andy.

He said: "We will have a wild hog run anytime. Old Ned has a claim on the wild hogs he never used. You can use them now." I told him I owned one of Wat Cannon's dogs—the one called Shep. He slammed his hand down on the table, saying: "He is the smartest wild hog dog I have ever known. Come here and stay all night anytime. We will have fun."

He ask: could I shoot? I told him I had graduated under Jack Prince, both rifle and pistol. " 'Nuff said. I'll try you out when we are through eating." I ask: "Will I have trouble with anyone resenting me traping?" He said: "If you do, come to me. Some times the Tick Bushers come in hunting hogs. They are a dirty lot. Those Newbys and Skinners are a mean lot. If you run into them don't even talk to them. They are always looking for trouble." I didn't talk of my troubles with them.

When we were outside he tried my rifle, hitting everything he shot at. A tree lark settled on the rail fence close to fifty yards away. He ask: "Are you good enough to get that bird?" When I shot the bird tumbled to the ground. He slapped me on the back, and said: "Jack has really trained you. That's damn good." He walked with me for a quarter of a mile to show me a trail to Sewanee that would save fully a quarter of a mile.

These people became to be the best friends I had in the mountains. Andy and I became to be close friends as we trapped and hunted for the next three months.

On the way home I thought of what Grandpa had told me—not to talk about what I learned around the mountaineers. I was still puzzled over Andy's Mama, a white woman, and why Alf Cannon was being so selfish. I knew I hadn't better talk of this to nobody. No Negro knew about Andy.

It all came clear now what Grandpa meant the day he talked about Wat Cannon. Alf Cannon was the nigger that they had defended. That was why he kept himself away from other Negroes. I knew I would learn more about this in time. Meanwhile, I would seal my lips and not talk to no one about it.

When I got home I had to take a reprimanding from

Mama. The gossipers had been to see her, telling her how I had squandered money the night before, showing off before the new girl. I said: "I spent a dollar-and-thirty cents the entire night."

Mama said: "That could feed us for a week." She demanded my pistol, telling me not to see the girl anymore. That night was the first time I refused to obey her. I ask her not to deny me of my guns: "I am not going to be without them, so please don't ask me to. I don't care what the niggers say about me anymore. They are going to respect me from now on." Mama slapped me across the mouth, saying: "Shut up." I went to bed soon. That was the end of it.

Next morning at five o'clock with twenty steel traps on my back, I headed for the Atkins home.

Andy and I went into the canyon. He told me about some people that done hunting further down the lowlands near Sherwood—four miles from our canyon. I wanted to see if I couldn't buy their furs at a profit.

It was strange to think Andy knew every mountaineer between his home and Sherwood, but not one person in Sewanee. He hadn't ever been in Sewanee. I make a deal with him to run my traps on Sunday for half the catch. I couldn't do this and be back for Sunday School which I hadn't missed but once in three years.

Two days later I had installed twenty dead polecats, some honey holes and some snares. Andy knew every trail in each fork on two small canyons farther west that had no names. He and I made a trip five miles down the lowlands toward Sherwood. He was liked by everybody. No one treated him like he was a Negro.

206

We went to five homes where I collected seventy pelts, four skunks, some coons, but no possums, at the cost of fourteen dollars. Many of the pelts were skinned wrong—split and not cased. I showed the boys how to case pelts, and said I would be back in three weeks.

Everything was in my favor. Trapping was good for skunks. In ten days I had thirty pelts. I lost all the coons in the canebrake on the stream where they roved. A coon in a trap had no defense against a wild hog. I would find only a coon's leg in a trap. Wild hogs go out to find food at dawn like all wild animals, and they would beat me to the traps. I gave up coons. I didn't care to fatten hogs on coons.

All the skunks were of a large breed, and most black. Half of the ones I caught were appraised extra-large. Narrow stripe skunk pelts had a value of one dollar and a quarter, short pelts two dollars, and black pelts up to three dollars. Ten foxes was all I caught. They sold for three dollars a piece. I caught over a hundred and fifty skunks out of that one canyon in three months.

Andy and I were in the mountains every hour I was around. He was always a bit of a curiosity to me. He never spoke unless I ask him something. When he saw an animal, he would yell: "Hoo Wee." He didn't care to shoot, and would rather tell me to shoot it.

One morning we met Alf Cannon on the trail. He passed us without speaking. I spoke to him, but he didn't speak at all. I ask Andy: didn't he and his father speak? He shook his head and quickened his steps to get away from me. I never mentioned his father again. I knew he realized he was a man without a country.

Mr. and Mrs. Atkins were the kindest people I have

ever known. They made me welcome at all times. John Atkins almost went wild over my pack of dogs. I had to hunt with him once every week. When he discovered Shep that was said to be the smartest hog dog in the mountains, he planned we would do some wild hog hunting.

He said: "There is a boar in the canyon that everybody has tried to get. He will weigh four hundred pounds. I know Shep will track him down. That dog knows how to get that boar out of a cave once we find it. You and Andy and I will get that devil. I have seen that dog work."

He also said: "I have seen that hog. He is a mustang—his ears have been frozen off. He has no marks, so he is anybody's hog that gets him. I want him. Many people has tried for five years. He gets away. They call him the devil. He has killed several dogs because they didn't know how to take care of themselves. He won't fool that old Sheperd dog."

The third week in January, just after a heavy snow, John Atkins said: "That snow is melting. Bring your dog tomorrow, and we will get that devil hog. Tracking will be easy." That was to be my first hog hunt. It was eight o'clock in the morning when I arrived at his house. There were two young men name Russell there that lived down the canyon. They were to join the hunt.

At the edge of the canebrake John found big tracks. He said: "You will see what a smart dog you own." He tied a rope around Shep's neck, holding the rope like a leash. Shep began to switch his tail, moving along and sniffing with his nose. Soon he was on the right trail.

We covered at least a mile, meandering along the side

of the mountain, and eventually stopping at a rocky ravine where there was a cave about eight feet wide and three feet high. Shep stood whining and wagging his tail.

John said: "He is in there. I didn't know this cave was here." He taken the rope off Shep, and said: "Shep will bring him out. I've seen him do it. You send him in." He told us all to get on a boulder.

I told Shep to go get him. He went in the cave wagging his tail. Soon, he let out some barks. We could hear the hogs snorting. Shep came out, running for his life with the hogs after him. There were at least ten. The big boar was in front.

Shep and the boar went down the mountain. The other hogs went around the ledge. This was a break for us. The boar had separated himself from the other hogs. This saved us of much trouble and danger.

When Shep got to a level place he began circling with the boar right after him. After a couple of circles the boar stopped, turning to keep his eyes on Shep. Shep stopped and walked towards the boar. As he would rush at Shep and snarl at him, Shep would leap aside and repeat the same action over again. I said: "John, I am going to shoot him before he hurts my dog." John said: "No, let Shep work him, so as to take the pertness out of him. Then, he won't want to run. When he is tired we will urge him close to the road and kill him."

Just at that moment the boar charged at Shep running him onto a patch of snow. Shep slipped flat on his stomach. The hog rushed him, slashing at him too high. Shep didn't come to his feet as the boar expected. He rolled away, keeping close on the ground. The boar snared so hard it caused Shep to spin around. Shep came to his feet, starting again to antagonize the boar.

John Atkins yelled: "Did you see that dog? How he out-smarted that hog? I tell you that is the smartest dog ever in these mountains." I leaped off my boulder, telling John: "I am going to kill that boar now. He won't kill my dog." As I approached he started to run down the mountain. John yelled: "Don't let him get away."

The boar raced to the bottom of the canyon, through the canebrake, and up the other side over the fork to the other canyon. Shep and I ran after him within fifty yards.

As we crossed the trail of Natural Bridge, John Cooksey had to leap out of the trail to keep the boar from running over him. I knew he was looking for moonshine and not hogs. He yelled something at me. I was running too fast with my rifle over my head to hear what he said.

The hog headed up the canyon toward the Two Mile Branch waterfall. There he got boxed in. The zero weather a few days before had frozen huge icicles that blocked the passage under the first waterfall. The ledge also was covered with ice. He skidded and lost his footing, falling off twenty feet down onto the ice below, landing on his back. He was paralyzed and couldn't get to his feet again.

As I started down to shoot him I heard a voice from the other side of the canyon, saying: "Don't touch that hog, nigger. That is our hog. What in the hell are you doing over here? You don't have no claim on hogs. We are going to take that one." There were six of them, four with dogs on leashes, the other two with rifles. They were a part of the Tick Bush gang.

I thought of what Jack had told me—that they would kill me as quick as they would a mad dog. I dropped behind a boulder and told them not to raise their guns if they wanted to live. They had started to raise their guns to their shoulders, when Newsom, one of them, said: "Skinner, that nigger can really shoot." They brought their guns down, as Andy caught up with me. He wanted to know what the argument was. I told him: "They want to take the hog." He said: "John will be here in a minute. He will tell them off."

Soon, John and one of the Russells came. Andy told John what was up. The gang had gone to the hog and shot it. John be angry. He said: "Ely, give me your gun." I said: "No, they started to shoot me, and I am not taking no chances." He: "I don't need no gun. I'll let them know who runs this canyon."

He went to them. There was an argument. John knocked one of them down. The others backed away, and went up the mountain. They yelled back at me: "Nigger, we are going to kill you and all your damn dogs."

We went to the hog. He was a whopper. He look to be six feet long. John Atkins was excited over our catch. The hog weighed fully four hundred pounds. There were many stories about that boar. He had killed over a dozen hog dogs and had even challenged men.

I taken off his tusks that was three inches long and sharp as blades. We four using a pole through his feet tied together tugged him a quarter of a mile to the top of Natural Bridge. John and Andy went to get the team and wagon. The Russell boy and I had to stay with the hog until they came back.

The boy wanted to know why those fellows didn't like me. I explained that I am a Negro, and I hunted in their area. "They just don't like Negroes." He said: "Andy's father is a black man." He pointed at Alf Cannon's house down the canyon. "Everybody likes Andy."

This was my opportunity to find the answer I wanted to know. I ask: "How come Alf Cannon was not lynched when it was discovered he had been dealing with a white woman?" This is forbidden in the South, I am told.

He said: "I was a small boy when Andy was born. Nobody talked about it after the first month he was born. When they discovered he was a black baby, it started a hell of a stink. My Pa told us boys about it. There was a lot of men from Sherwood came here to hang Alf, but the three Cannon brothers turned those fellows back, threatening to kill anybody that touched Alf.

"In the time of slavery the Cannons had a small plantation down in the lowlands. They once owned most of these canyons. After the slaves were freed the six they owned never left them. Alf is one of the sons. He grew up with the three young Cannons. He was just like one of the family. Andy's mother was hired to work for the Cannons. This is how she and Alf got to be close.

"She told the nobbers that she done what she did for money. She just got caught, and they shouldn't harm Alf. She told them it was her fault, that he hadn't raped her. Those Cannons were a tough sort. They made the nobbers scram.

"All the people here joined with the Cannons. Everybody honored her for being honest. Alf went somewhere and got him a black woman. The Cannons gave him that farm. He has raised a family. Everybody in this canyon likes Alf. He don't have no black friends. Five years later John Atkins married Andy's mother. John has raised Andy and he has a son of his own. He and Alf Cannon are friends. John would kill anybody that bothered Andy.

"You know Sewanee has their own way of law for their black people. I have been told that the uppish white people there thinks more of the black people than they do of the poor white people. They say they don't call you people niggers like they do in other places in the South.

"We are not supposed to talk about this. I have told you because you are like one of us. Don't talk of it again to no one. It is our business. There are just two kinds of people here—man and woman."

I stood for several minutes looking down at the smoke from Alf Cannon's chimney. I couldn't hardly believe what my ears had heard. Alf Cannon was the luckiest Negro in the South.

That day was the twentieth of January, 1912. I had killed the largest game of my hunting experience, and had heard the strangest story of truth that could be told of the South. I envied Andy. He didn't have no Negroes around to call him a bastard.

Shep and I had built a reputation. As much as twice a week we helped someone run down hogs. He was the only dog that would go in the caves and bring them out. I was glad to do it for them because this canyon was the only place in the South I have ever felt free.

CHAPTER
13

During those months I was so much in the mountains there had been much activity in Sewanee. There was a lot of entertainment given for the Negroes—such as, cakewalks and festivals. I had gone to four such events with my sweetheart. Having money to spend, I was wearing tailor-made clothes, and I was the only boy that sported new clothes.

The secret had leaked out about my foster brother's ailment. It was the town talk of how I had made money enough to pay such a doctor bill. My stock had rose with the girls and older people, but not with the men and younger boys.

I had hunted nearly every night. I would rest three hours on return from my traps. I had an area of about seven miles to hunt. There were four canyons, and I would hunt each one night a week.

There was one canyon named Thump and Dick. I gave up this canyon. It was rugged and heavily foliaged. I was frightened there one night so much that I never cared to hunt it again. All hunters held some fear of that canyon. Many distressing stories were told about it.

I had explored it twice in the daytime. There were many small caves, and many animal tracks that I just could not be sure whether they were dogs or huge cats or wild goats or even wild hogs. It was narrow and deep and had a good stream. No one lived within two miles of it. There were no trails through it—just around the rim.

As I went down from the rim, I heard a woman scream not far away. At least, I thought it was a woman. I yelled as to answer. The scream came again. This time it was across the canyon. The hounds struck a hot trail, and soon began to bay on the other side of the canyon.

I started across through the thick bushes. I had gone fifty yards when a fight started, and then everything went silent. The next thing I realized all of my dogs were around me with their tails between their legs, whining. This was a most weird moment for me. The most strange thing of all was stumbling over my dogs as they hovered around me. This is one experience that I don't have a sound answer to.

Speaking of experience—the mountaineers had many home remedies. This one may sound rare that I participated in—taking the fat off a skunk and rendering the fat to oil, it could be given to children as a remedy for croupe and whooping cough. It was also supposed to be good for rhumatics. This I will agree with. I had held the rifle in my right hand so much that year rhumatism had affected my index finger and thumb. Every morning it would be so stiff I would hope to catch a skunk, because before I would finish skinning it my fingers would be supple. I rendered many pounds of skunk fat, and traded it to the mountaineers for furs.

This led me, regardless of my discomforts, to analyze the skunk. I found he lived mostly on insects like bees and yellow jackets, and on various herbs, as well as on meat. I arrived at this decision—the skunk could be called a bit of a pharmaceutical animal. I was having many of the girls to slip out at night and go hunting with me. No one of them talked about the skunk odor.

My little brother had been sent away to school. This had stopped me from having Negro fights. My trouble with the sagers also lessened, because most of the young ones wanted to sell me their furs when they got any.

I did run into trouble with the Tick Bush gang at Two Mile Branch on Washington's Birthday. Jessie, my girl-friend, had slipped out to hunt with me. The dogs had treed what we thought was a coon. I told her to hold my rifle while I hooked up my carbide light.

I heard the click of the hammer of my rifle as she said: "Don't point that gun at him. Drop it." I came to my feet to see there were four men, one with a shotgun. Skinner let his gun down, staring at her. Newsom said: "That's our game. Our dogs treed it." I ask her to give me the gun. She refused, saying: "I can shoot and I will. Let them have the coon. No coon is worth the trouble."

If ever I surrendered to anything that hurt that was it. I put my lantern out. We went in to the undergrowth fifty yards away, and waited for them to get the animal out, so my dogs would come back to us. It was a house cat. I heard them cursing it as they shot it.

This was the first time I knew Jessie understood about a gun. She told me she had been a tomboy with her three brothers, and had hunted and fished with them.

Then, she said: "You are the man I want. I love everything you do. We are going to get married, and we will be the finest colored couple Sewanee ever had. These moun-

216

tains are a part of you. I love them, too. I want to become to be the school teacher here. You will be my first student. We will hunt and have fun."

We made plans for our wedding to take place the second Sunday in May. That would be when the colored advocates of the hard-shell, foot-washing Baptist goes to Beans Creek for a foot-washing. That was far from her home in the town of Pelham. We planned to surprise everybody. She would be leaving the first of March.

That night she persuaded me not to hunt alone anymore.

Next day Henry Prince stopped me, and said I should stop carrying money on me to buy furs. "Take a check book. There is some talk of robbing you. It means they will ambush you."

Two days later I got a letter from Meridian, Mississippi, from a little nurse I had dated the previous summer saying I was the father of her expected baby. She said I should send for her and marry her.

This grew to be an increasing problem by the first of March. I went to my old men friends for advice. I didn't know what to do with that kind of trouble. They all giggled and made fun of it, saying: "What a man!" Hugh Hill said: "Let the gals worry about it." It wasn't that easy for me. It was a burden I had to carry alone.

On the first of March the Gibsons sent word to me to come down to their house to get some furs. This was at the foot of the Winchester road. They had twelve dollars worth.

Coming back at Poplar Springs, a wild turkey crossed ahead of me. I ran after it, trying to get a shot. I came upon a saddle. It was a find. I hadn't seen anyone with one like it except Mr. Rosborough. I carried it home. It was much weatherbeaten. I cleaned it up with saddle soap and hung it on the front porch, hoping someone would claim it.

Many people came to see it but for a month no one claimed it. Uncle Rufus Mosley offered ten dollars for it, and I sold it to him with the understanding that if the owner should turn up, I would refund his money.

I taken my girlfriend's advice to get someone to hunt with me. In Green View canyon I found paper tied on bushes, reading: "Nigger Stay Out Of The Mountains." I couldn't find no colored boys that wanted to hunt.

The second of March Will Roe, who lived next door, had three hogs he was to kill. One of them jumped the fence and ran into the woods. He had hired my cousin Will, a young fellow, to help him. I saw them chasing the hog. I could see they would never catch him.

I told Will: "I will shoot him." He said: "Alright. If you can with a pistol." I got within thirty feet, got a good aim at his head, and the shot was good. Will came to me, saying: "I'll hunt with you, if you will teach me to shoot like that." I said: "That's a deal. I'll teach you all I can."

For the next two weeks he went with me every day. All he wanted to do was shoot the pistol at every tree he passed. I found he wanted to be a big bully. He was arrogant and full of hate. I couldn't see why—he was very dark, and his mother and father worshipped him. He was twenty years old.

His family hadn't lived in Sewanee more than a year. He didn't care for women. He liked to gamble which caused him to get beat up a couple of times. We confided to each other our grievances and revenges.

I was surprised when he told me of Negroes that had planned to rob me, and somehow I missed their plans. That, of course, made me feel closer to him. By the end of two weeks we had agreed we would be as close as two people could be. We would stick together, no matter what. I didn't know too much about him, but I did know I needed someone for a friend.

The season was over for trapping and hunting. I sized up my condition like this—Scott, my foster-brother, was now the picture of health. He had started to work. All bills were paid. I had cleared—by buying or catching furs, gathering nuts and herbs, selling wood—close to four hundred dollars since September. I had bought Mama a coat, a suit and two pair of shoes—fifteen dollars. I had two new suits, three pair of shoes, some shirts and socks. This was also my first time to wear B. V. D.'s. I had fifty dollars in the bank. Mama had twenty dollars. I also had the guns and watches I was holding for six dollars.

Everything was fine except for the baby trouble. That was bad enough, but trouble increased nearer home. Hugh Hill gave a party the first week in April. I taken Will with me. No one seemed to like him. He tried to drink all the whiskey. He got drunk. I didn't know he had stolen my gun before we left home. He decided to shoot Uncle Bill Jones for no reason. I knocked the gun up, as it went off. Uncle Will accused me of teaching his son to be a desperado. He said that since Will Junior had been around me all he talked about was killing people. He said: "Don't ever come to my house. You were born for no good." This really sunk in. I said from that minute: "Damn all Negroes, all relatives and all sagers." I became to be as evil as a person could feel. I decided I didn't want no friends. I would fight my own battles by myself.

I taken my job back with the Calmores. The ten dollars a week sure was slow pay, as I had been making faster money.

The morning after the Titanic sunk Miss Dora Calmore told me Major Butts went down with it. All of Sewanee was in mourning.

That same day I went to Father Eastern and told him about my troubles. I asked him: "What should I do? I am accused four ways. I am threatened to be prosecuted by one man, and another has threatened to shoot me if I don't marry his daughter. I don't believe either woman is carrying my child." Father said: "Wait until these children are born. That is the only way to know."

Neither one of the families wanted to listen to this. That is when I told Mama. She lay me low with her tongue. I felt more friendless than ever. She didn't sympathize no way, although she did not want me to marry anyone. By this time I didn't talk to no one. I was ready to fight anybody. I felt ashamed think I had created a bastard to suffer like I had.

I was still expecting someone to come back for the saddle. I had told Jack Prince about it. He said: "The Tick Bushers never had enough money to buy a saddle like that. Come to me if they come to claim it." I said: "I will unless they came with guns. If so, I will meet them with a gun, and I am not waiting to be shot first. I want to kill all of them."

Jack said: "I think you had better let me take your guns, or get that idea out of your mind." Henry, Jack's son, said: "Dad's right, Ely, fighting won't do." I agreed I was wrong. Jack said: "They have to come by here if they come. I will be watching." I felt good to think I had a friend.

I wanted to go to Constable Dakin, but he didn't like me. He hadn't bothered me about the shootings at McFarling, but he knew all the high-up white people favored me. He would have to go to both my counselmen before he could arrest me.

The next night I taken my hounds over to Shakerag Hollow to let them have some exercise. There was a fox chase on. The fox came close to my dogs. They became excited, and got into the chase. They had done this before. It always made the mountaineers angry, because an English hound was so fast it would put a gray fox in a hole within an hour.

Two days later I was sawing wood when five of the Tick Bushers rode up to my gate. Three of them had rifles. I thought they were coming to claim the saddle. Hell seemed to surge through me. All I wanted was for somebody to start something. I wasn't going to yield to nothing.

One of them got off his horse, and came in the gate. He said: "We came here to look at your dogs' teeth. They got on our fox run the other night. We found three of our sheep killed yesterday. Your dogs was in our district. We want to see if your dogs have sheep wool in their teeth." I said: "If that is what you want to do, go and look for yourself." My rifle was sitting behind the tree close to me.

He went to the dogs' pen and opened the gate. White and Laura, my two breed dogs went up to him. He looked in their mouths came back out, went to his mule, untied his rifle and came back in the gate.

I ask: "What are you going to do with that gun?" He said: "I am going to kill the dogs they got sheep wool in their teeth." I stepped foward with my rifle at hip-action, saying: "The first man shoots a dog, I shoot him. Drop that rifle." He did.

Just then Jack Prince rode up. He listened for a minute to what I was saying. I told them: "It is not your job to kill other peoples' dogs. You go and get Dakin, the Constable."

Jack ask: "What's going on?" One of them said: "You are in time to see a nigger killed." Jack said: "Don't try anything if you don't want to die. He's not bluffing—he'll shoot all three of you before you get a gun up to shoot back. He is quick as lightning with a rifle. You go like he asks, and get Dakin."

Jack came in the yard, and sat between two piles of wood. He said: "I want to be here when they come back. I saw them as they passed my house. I had to saddle up before I could start. I thought they were headed here. I don't blame you for not letting them destroy your fine dogs. They are just begrudging. All they do is make trouble."

They rode up again and Dakin was with them. Dakin dismounted and opened the gate. I walked to the porch which placed me direct in front of them. Dakin said: "Boy, you are crazy. Don't you know better than to threaten people with a gun. I am going to examine those dogs. If they have wool in their teeth I will shoot them. That's the law."

I spoke then, saying: "Mr. Dakin, you can examine my dogs, but you won't kill no dog of mine. Any man kill a dog of mine I will kill him. The law is the dog must be gotten rid of. Each of those dogs is pedigreed and registered at the Mississippi Kennels. They are English hounds valued from twenty-five to seventy-five dollars a dog. I would return them back to the Kennels."

He said: "Do you respect what I represent?" I said: "No, not when you are going to destroy my property of value. I mean to protect every damn thing I own, law or no law."

One of the others said: "I am going to kill that nigger." He started to lift his rifle from the saddle. I yelled at him: "Don't raise that gun at me. Put it down. Do you think I am going to let them shoot me." Dakin looked back at them, and shook his head.

I didn't know Mama had come out of the house onto the porch back of me until Dakin said: "Mat, the white people gave you that boy to raise. Is this the way you raised him—not to have any respect for white people or for law?"

At that moment, Mama reached over my shoulder and snatched my rifle, slamming the stock down on the banister and breaking it. She said: "Pull your shirt off. I am going to give you the licking of your life."

No one had noticed Jack setting by the wood pile. As I was pulling my shirt over my head, I heard Jack shout: "Don't one of you raise a gun. I mean don't attempt to shoot that boy."

Mama taken the hitch rein to my holster—a one-inch sea-grass rope. It had a wire wrapped end that held the ravel. She lashed me at least twenty lashes. Every lash brought blood that ran to my heels. I know she didn't notice the effect until it was over.

She said to Dakin: "Now you can see that I didn't raise him to be so important towards you white people." That statement drove me into a tantrum. I started cursing them, calling them all kinds of sons of bitches, and telling them that as soon as I could get a gun I would kill them. Jumping up and down swearing, I said: "I will never stop until I kill you. I don't want to live if I have to crawl to you poor white sagers."

Jack said to Dakin: "Take these men away now." Jack and Dakin hadn't spoken in five years. Dakin got on his old black mare, and they rode away. I went to Jack and thanked him for saving my life. He said to Mama: "You almost got the boy killed. Wet a towel and wipe the blood off his back. I am going to take Ely with me. I can't leave him hear with no protection."

We left. Jack said: "I want to talk to your counselmen." I said: "We will go to Father Eastern." He said: "They will be back. Since Dakin favored them he had no right to bring them with him. He was just going to stand there and let them shoot you. He don't like you. I am going to report this to the officials of Sewanee."

At Father's house Jack explained why he was there with me. After he had finished Father ask me how did I feel about it? I told him all I wanted to do was kill them as soon I got a rifle. Nothing Father could say would change my mind. I repeated this time after time.

Then, he said: "Don't talk. I want to think a while." He stood looking out the window for a few minutes. When he spoke, he said: "My son, I think this can be a solution to all of your problems. Go away for a while—at least six months. You are most bitter. Leave today. Do you have money?" I said: "Yes. Sixty dollars." He said: "Write me, so I can have a Father to look after you." I told him I would.

I saw at once that Father was right. A little time could play a great part in my problems. Then, he said: "I give you this advice. Do refrain from being so determined. Be brave enough to be patient." This I never forgot. It was to me the most wonderful blessing I ever received. That was the last time I saw Father Eastern.

I went to Mother Richerson's home where Aunt Ada worked. Jack had advised me to remain in the Corporation. He said: "Those sagers might come back, since Dakin favored them. When you are ready to leave, I will put you on the train."

When I got to Aunt Ada's, Uncle Doss was home. The rain that morning had caused him to come home. I told them of what had happened, and asked Uncle Doss to go and get my clothes. I wrote down what I wanted him to bring. He didn't return until nine o'clock that night. He explained that many riders had passed Mama's house until eight o'clock. Dakin had come and talked to Mama, telling her not to talk to no colored people about your trouble. Not any of them knew about it.

Uncle Doss said: "I'm going to take you to Cowan. There is a work-car at the top of Poplar Spring canyon. It's a heavy one. I think we can get it on the track. The grade starts down there. It will skate down to Cowan. We will leave hear at two o'clock. No one will be stirring at that hour. We can skirt the town, go through the S.M.A. campus, and then head for the railroad. Get some sleep. You will need it."

I found myself feeling close to him for the first time. He said: "I wish some of them would try to stop us. I brought your pistol with me. I would like to put a blaze under them sagers." I knew how he hated sagers. I had lost all the desire to fight. After receiving the blessing from Father Eastern, I couldn't sleep for thinking of how the outer world would be.

Before we left, Aunt Ada said: "I am glad to see you go. I have for the last two years worried about you. I have expected to hear of you having trouble or shooting somebody. I have wished that you hadn't ever seen a gun." Uncle Doss said: "If it hadn't been that he is as good a shot as he is, he wouldn't be living."

As I stood there I began to feel lonely for the first since I had talked to my mother at the waterfall five years before. It seemed I was being stripped of invisible clothing, and my soul was bare to the world. I suppose all people feel that way when leaving a world they love like I loved Sewanee and the mountains.

I had always believed that those ten thousand acres represented the Greatness of God. It wasn't long before it was definitely confirmed that my feeling and thought of Sewanee were true. I didn't know at this time that the greatness of Sewanee would be my guide on the life journey, walking the path of tradition.

226

On our way to the railroad we didn't meet a person. I told Uncle Doss that I could go by myself. We had a hard time getting the heavy cart on the rails. I looked back at Uncle Doss, knowing he had helped me get started away. He was as glad to see me go as anyone. The cart moved very slow until I passed the home of the Sisters of St. Mary —then the grade dropped. I hated to leave those mountains I knew so well. They were a part of me: would I ever see them again? I loved every foot of that beautiful area. I was praying some, too.

I realized the cart was increasing speed every second. I became worried how I could stay on that flatcar going around curves at such a rate of speed. I almost lost my suitcase when it slid away from me. Holding on with one hand I just barely caught the hand-grip with two fingers of the other hand to hold it long enough for the cart to straighten. It swung back against me, almost pushing me off the cart.

I could see that I had a straight strip of road for a distance. I knew there was no getting off of the cart until I was at the end of the track. All at once I knew my life was facing a gamble. I knew the surges would come from each side, so I quickly placed my suitcase in the center of the cart. I lay across it hooking toes to one side and holding the other with my hands.

Soon, I was in the bends of the road. It was a struggle to hold on. The cart was flying, and I didn't see how it could stay on the track. This lasted for about ten minutes which seemed like an eternity to me. Trying to look ahead of me made it hard to breathe. I hadn't ever rode this fast, even on the train. I can't say I was scared. Really I didn't care too much about what could happen. I knew this—I am free and my own man. I said several times; "I have got to make it."

All of a sudden I came out on the rim of a mountain. I saw Cowan below. I knew I had made it. There was one more trying curve, almost like a horse-bend. This one I had to hold on with my toes. I was tired. I relaxed for a few moments. When I passed over the tunnel of the N and C Mainline I tightened my grip on the cart. Again the surge was on, stronger than ever. I managed to last it through.

The road gradually came down parallel to the Mainline track for a mile. The cart was still traveling at a high rate of speed. I knew I had to stop it some way, or jump off before reaching the switch. I had on heavy-sole shoes. I chanced falling off by sitting on the edge so as to press my foot against the wheel as a brake. This checked the cart effectively until my foot was burning painfully. The cart stopped about fifty yards from the switch.

I tried to get the cart off the track. I couldn't. I knew there wouldn't be a train along until seven o'clock in the morning. I left it, and walked to the station, wondering why did Uncle Doss put me on a cart without a brake on it? He was a railroad man and knew this road like a book. Did he mean to kill me this way? I wouldn't ever know because I wouldn't ever see him again.

Anyhow, I was alive. My foot was paining when I reached the station. No one except the ticket agent was in the station. When I walked in I looked at the clock on the wall: it read three-twenty-five. I had come eight miles in twenty minutes on a flat cart down the winding road of the mountains. I sat down in the sitting room for a few minutes to think. All I could think of was that the mountains had taken care of me until now.

The agent was much like most of the poor class of white people. He poked his head through the window, and said: "Where did you come from this time of morning?" I said: "What time will the next train be coming through to Nashville?" He said: "Cannon Ball will be here in the next thirty minutes. If she is on time she will stop. If she is late she won't."

I went to the window, and ask him to give me a ticket to Waxahochie, Texas. "I want to catch this next train." He said: "Nigger, are you running from trouble? What have you done? How did you get here this time of morning? I haven't heard a sound of a horse's foot. You must have walked a distance."

I ask again: "Will you sell me a ticket?" He hesitated a moment, and then said: "Yes, that's my job. You are just a boy. I could be wrong, but every time I have sold a ticket to Texas this time of morning they comes looking for them."

I went in the toilet room and changed clothes. My shoe I had used to brake with the sole was burned badly, and was no good. All I had left for shoes was a pair of dancing pumps. I put them on, and dressed in a blue serge suit, boxed-back, peg-tops, pants of soft white flannel, and a white hat with a purple band like the Sewanee students wore.

When I ask for my ticket, I ask the agent how long it would be before the train arrived. He looked at me, and said: "She will be here in the next two minutes. I will try to stop her." Then he said: "You are a Sewanee nigger. I can tell the way they dress. They all are high-collared and proud—just like them damn white people up their on that mountain. They don't have no use for a poor white man, and I don't have any use for them."

He said: "I have signaled for her to stop. Get out there because she will barely stop. You might have to swing on." The train almost passed the station before stopping. I caught the last coach with the help of the porter taking my suitcase from me as I kept up with the moving train. I swung on.

That was the first time I had seen a pullman coach. The porter looked at my ticket, and said: "Follow me. You go to the day coach." We had to go through many pull-mans before we reached a chair car. The porter said: "You are a Sewanee boy." I said: "Yes." He said: "I know them when I see them. No one wears a hat like that except them. I have had their teams many times." He placed my suitcase in the rack, and said: "This is your chair." I sat down, and he went to the next coach.

I looked around me. Everybody was white. No colored anywhere. I knew the porter had made a mistake in thinking that I was a white school boy—evidently, a cadet.

I didn't have any intention of making my identity known just then. I pulled my hat down tight as I could on my head to keep my sandy, curly hair from showing too much. No one would discover that I was a Negro. In the morning I would go to the colored coach.

I lay back in the chair, and began to review the night's events. Everything in the world had changed within the last three days. So many times I heard whispers coming from somewhere, saying: "Out there, out there . . . I am

230

out there. I know I am going to see, hear, and do things I never knew of. In Texas I won't be called a bastard or a clabber or a nigger like that sager ticket agent in Cowan called me."

I thought of what a Negro had said in Alabama—that a Southern sager could smell Negro blood in a person no matter how white he was. I remembered how quick that agent discovered I was a Negro the moment I walked into the sitting room. The porter, a Negro himself, didn't know I was a Negro.

I had heard Ann say that when you are travelling act as in Rome. She travelled two days in a white coach, and no one knew the difference. I finally decided that I didn't ask to be there. I had obeyed the porter. I was not trying to pass for white. All they could do was tell me to go to the Negro car.

I began to think of every friend I had left in Sewanee. I began to wonder what I would do to make a living in Texas. I would miss Mr. Calmore, Mr. Rosborough, Jack Prince and Johnny McKay. I hadn't told them good-bye. Those friends had been much of a part in my life.

Scott, Mama's oldest son, was improving with his health. He would soon go to work on the new church project. I would send money when I made some. She could sell my gun, and my fine dogs.

As I looked out the window I could see dawn was approaching. That had been a sacred hour when I was in the mountains. That was the last time I held any thought of the life I had left behind me.

The porter came through, and said: "Nashville in fifteen minutes."

Publisher's Note

The University of the South—the "corporation" to which Ely Green refers—was one of the utopian educational projects of nineteenth-century America; and unlike many others it has continued to the present. In Ely's day it was enjoying a "golden age," with medical, law, dental, nursing, and engineering departments in addition to the college, theological school, and military academy which still survive.

When Mr. Green refers to a tightly regulated society, he is not exaggerating. The Tennessee legislature granted a remarkable charter to the University in 1858, which conferred upon it broad municipal authority plus police power. Government was in the hands of the Trustees: some fifteen Episcopal bishops of Southern dioceses, an equal number of priests, and thirty elected laymen. The Vice-Chancellor —Dr. Benjamin Lawton Wiggins during Ely's day—was in effect the governor of a 10,000-acre domain, exercising control by the ability to grant, withhold, or cancel leaseholds.

Ely's chronology is not to be taken as history though his sequence of events is generally true. He remembers that ground was broken for All Saint's Chapel one fall with the cornerstone to be laid next spring, but he places these events several years after 1904 and 1905. The military academy was military, but its formal name was the "Grammar School" until 1908. Sewanee often defeated "Georgie Teck," but these games always took place in Atlanta.

In the original manuscript there were no paragraphs, no chapter divisions, no quotation marks, little punctuation. These have been added, though the flavor of the original was so appealing—with its constant reminder of the author's prodigious accomplishment in writing it with almost no formal education—that there was a temptation to make no alterations at all. The present draft of the manuscript is the third, the first having been destroyed and the second stolen. A photographic copy of the handwritten manuscript will be placed in the library of the School of Theology at Sewanee and the original handwritten version in the archives of the duPont Library, University of the South.

Ely Green's Sewanee is a place in his memory, not an historical reconstruction done by an archaeologist. Many of the houses are gone. The modern structures more or less on the sites of the Bartons, the Barnwells, and Mrs. Tucker's Palmetto received their present names from Vice-Chancellor Alexander Guerry, "Father's oldest boy." Breslin Tower's chimes sound the hours just as Ely heard them. The corporation fence is gone, along with the other barriers of which he speaks.

The people of Ely's Sewanee were named, though not spelled, the way he remembers, except for three or four families whose names were changed for publication. Many of the names of Ely's friends are as familiar on the Mountain today as sixty years ago.

Ely's mountains remain with their chalybeate springs, laurel, coons and possums, though the ginseng beds are sel-

dom harvested and the boars—and the people—are gone
from Lost Cove.

Most of the "near-miss" words used by the author are
sufficiently clear from the context. Here are a few which
might need explanation:

aristocrats: this is the author's own terminology for families
    connected with the University.
carter: cotta; white vestment worn over the cassock.
clabber: clabber-brained or half-witted.
clevic: chalybeate or mineral water; also "clebric."
corporation: the fenced-in portion of the University do-
    main, the central campus, about 1,000 acres.
estate: premises of one family, a leasehold; not in common
    usage today.
Frenzy: Forensic Hall, a frame building in which college
    dances and oratorical contests were held; now marked
    by a stone sundial.
Fedville: Fayetteville, Tennessee.
gensand: ginseng root, a flowering herb still commanding
    a high price for medicinal qualities.
quiene: quinine.
sager: mountaineer, covite.
scrip: paper issued by the University in lieu of money dur-
    ing times of bank failure and depression; also script.
Tick Bush: a community southeast of the University prop-
    erty line.
toten: carrying home leftovers of food was not considered

stealing and doubtless originated in the absence of re-
frigeration.

umberallow: umbrella.

Afterword

Nearly everything was perfect. The boy's father and grandfather were of good Southern stock, his mother diligent and loving. He was healthy and intelligent and reared in a college community. Physically he was attractive, red-haired, medium-sized, wiry, and so well coordinated that he fought the boxing champ of the Tenth Cavalry Regiment to a draw at Camp Travis in 1918. He was a woodsman of great skill. With a rifle he could shoot the head off a bird in a treetop and with a pistol hit coins tossed in the air. He was diplomatic, courteous, articulate, retentive, determined, and courageous.

But—he did not become Secretary-General of the United Nations. He did not become United States Senator from Tennessee, or president of Standard Oil. He was, he tells us, a "half-white bastard." Technically he was black, even though he could "pass." Obstinately, he seldom chose to pass as white, except, he once told me, to save his life.

Implied here is the uniquely American question: Why, in this country, would being white be necessary to save one's life? In this document, written and rewritten over a lifetime, Ely Green answers that question.

Elisha Green was born September 11, 1893, near Sewanee, Tennessee, the site of the University of the South. His mother Lena was the daughter of Ned Green, swill hauler and privy cleaner, who remembered being sold on the block as a slave. At seventeen Lena was working for a family (which we have called Doane) that belonged to the white gentry of the small Episcopal community. Mrs. Doane, widow of a Confederate officer, had two daughters and two sons. Lena never positively confirmed to her son which of the brothers was his father.

Lena and her illegitimate child were taken in by next-door neighbors, "Doc" Richardson, a crippled druggist and confectioner, and his wife, whose residence was located where the university faculty club now stands. At the age of four, the youngster was baptized in the Richardson parlor in a formidable ceremony with university chaplain William Alexander Guerry, later Bishop of South Carolina, performing the rite, assisted by the then Bishop-Coadjutor of Tennessee, the Rt. Rev. Thomas Frank Gailor, always referred to by Ely as his godfather. Witnesses were Archdeacon William S. Claiborne and the Rev. Churchill Eastin. Certainly no effort was spared to compensate in heaven for what credentials the child may have lacked on earth.

The nickname Ely (pronounced like the English cathedral, *EE-lee*, and not like the inventor of the cotton gin) was bestowed early and used by him the rest of his life. A couple of years after his birth, his mother married Lee Miller, and Ely soon had a half-brother, Eddie. When Lena lay dying of tuberculosis in 1901 or 1902, she asked the woman who had reared her to take Ely, because "as he is" he had "no one." Matty Davis took the orphan, and Miller married again,

238

taking Eddie but not Ely into that union, though retaining an affectionate interest in his wife's son.

The double jeopardy of segregation from whites and ostracism by blacks did not impinge on his consciousness until he was turning nine. From school mascot and campus pet he entered an increasingly stormy adolescence. Clashes with white mountaineers (called by Ely "sagers") and black youths built up tensions. Finally in 1912, a week after the memorial service for his friend Major Archibald Butt, who had died heroically on the *Titanic*, Ely fled a brewing lynching and went to Waxahachie, Texas. Before long he was employed as houseboy and chauffeur by the town's leading banker, living on the premises of his new boss, Judge Oscar E. Dunlap. Young Ely found that the only safety for a black man lay in securing the protection of a respected white man, and he determined to win this respect in his own right by becoming a "man to the flag and a citerzen" in the Army. He went to France in 1918 with a stevedoring unit and worked on the docks of St. Nazaire. After repeated efforts to get to the front lines, he concluded that "the long arm of tradition"—the influence of Judge Dunlap—was keeping him out of combat.

Back in Texas after the war, he lasted only about three more years before some truly classic cases of police brutality drove him away. He chauffeured for a wildcatter in the new Texas oil fields, but again his breaking the color line brought him eye to eye with a hanging noose. He was "too black" for employment in the segregated oil fields and "too white" to be a Pullman porter.

He went to California, which remained his home for the rest of his life. He worked as valet and steward on private yachts, visiting Mexico, Panama, Brazil, Paraguay, Argentina, and Australia. In the Depression he was butler and caterer in the Beverly Hills area, tending private bar for such celebrities as the Barrymores, mainly John, and Mary Pickford. I asked him why he had not written of these years with the Hollywood stars. He answered with patience and dignity: "I can't think up stories. I can only write what happened. These people were my friends, and I can't tell on them. I have to tell the truth. I can't write anything else."

In World War Two Green worked in the defense industry. He records how he spearheaded the desegregation of a Lockheed aircraft plant, in which the company was willing to hire men regardless of color but the unions would not admit blacks. By 1960 he had retired on Social Security and was recalling the events of his up-and-down life.

He was then a man of nearly seventy, with no private income or assets who knew in his heart that he had a message. Like a composer whose music had never been played, a sculptor whose statue had never been seen, he was a gifted writer whose magnum opus had never been read.

In 1961 I received a letter signed Ely E. Green, saying that he understood I was interested in stories about Sewanee. He was writing his "memories" and wanted my advice. He explained that he had no school record, "owing to becoming much confused over having to be called a Negro. I having white brothers and a black brother." I replied that I was much interested, that as historiographer of the University of the South I was constantly seeking documentation on life at Sewanee.

Silence. Three years later—about Christmas, 1964—a man with sandy reddish hair came to my door, directed by his half-brother, the custodian of the student union half a block away. Would I like to see his book? He brought me a suitcase with six looseleaf notebooks of handwritten pages, not sequentially numbered. When he returned the following day, my wife had read much of this mass to me because I found the handwriting at first try barely legible. I pressed him about places and people familiar to me. He stunned me by saying: "I've shown my book to lots of people, but you are the first who's read it." He asked me to try to get his book published, and I agreed to do what I could. He went back to California, but not before I had driven him throughout the community, asking about buildings he described which no longer existed. His memory was phenomenal. The last area of competence I could imagine for myself was as a literary agent for an unknown, technically illiterate, writer. To convert this copy into typescript would itself be expensive, and yet I did want the original for the Sewanee archives.

I inquired further about the genesis of the document. Most of the extant 1,200 pages were at least a third revision. With only a few weeks of formal education from John Kennerly, Sewanee's Negro schoolteacher and janitor, young Ely received a few more months of solid instruction from Mrs. Charlotte Streeter, a retired teacher friend of his foster mother. His real schooling—the education which enabled him to bequeath his life story—is described simply. He said he went to school to "every man who would converse" with him.

The blow which propelled him toward self-education came in Texas, when at the age of twenty he was rejected by his love, a college graduate, because he had no diploma. Desperation took him to a friend of his employer—he was ashamed to talk to the Judge—and he was given a curriculum and texts which included a speller, a dictionary, a copy of the *National Geographic*, an atlas, and a book by Jack London. Judge Dunlap, when he found out, gave him a ledger, small tablets, and a fountain pen, bidding him note during the day words he did not understand. At night the Judge or his daughter held sessions of "definement" going over his day's crude diary. This early document, together with his scrapbook of World War One, was destroyed by a lady friend in the early twenties. A companion journal was borrowed by a white man for testimony in an oil lease royalty suit. The man won the case, but neglected to share his half-million-dollar settlement and failed to return the diary.

My neighbor in Sewanee, theologian FitzSimons Allison, met Mr. Green and listened to parts of the manuscript. He told his editor, Arthur Buckley of Seabury Press in New York, that I had something Seabury should see. The Sewanee section, edited by Mr. Buckley, was published in 1966 with an introduction by Lillian Smith as *Ely: An Autobiography*.

A stroke early in 1966 put Ely Green in the Veterans Hospital in Santa Monica, California. His speech was impaired, and he was never able to write again. In August, 1967, he married Beatrice McCarroll, a long-time friend, whose devoted care during his convalescence made it possible for him to be an outpatient. On their wedding trip back to Sewanee he was given a gala autographing party. At home in Santa Monica on April 27, 1968, he returned from a walk with "indigestion," which proved to be a fatal heart attack. He was survived by two daughters, whose mothers were sisters and, separately, the companions of his teen-age hunting trips in the Tennessee mountains. He left an estate of less than five thousand dollars, and of that, three thousand had come from his book. More than fifty reviewers paid such high tribute that his last days were enveloped in an aura of fulfillment, and the way was paved for publishing the manuscript in its entirety.*

It is the reader's privilege to doubt the accuracy of this document. We have documented thoroughly the Sewanee portion. Ninety-four persons in that section we have known personally, or known their children, or have verified in the Sewanee Archives. An older brother received a younger brother's name, a couple of occurrences were in the right season but the wrong year, but no significant faults have been found. A few names have been changed to protect descendents. *Ely: An Autobiography*, we believe, is as accurate as a seventy-year-old memory could make it.

Having established to our satisfaction basic veracity, there came the question of editing. Our aim, and that of Arthur Buckley, was to make the manuscript readable without distorting meaning, style, or flavor, without unnecessary interruption and without condescension. Paragraphing, minimum punctuation, and words obviously omitted were supplied. A few extraneous or repetitive words were deleted.

The author's impressive vocabulary came from hearing words rather than reading them. Some words appear in several versions: Episcopalian, colonel, lieutenant, and character gave him the most trouble. Ely spelled phonetically and

*In 1970 the University of Massachusetts Press published Ely Green's complete memoir under the title *Ely: Too Black, Too White*. This Afterword is an abridged version of the Foreword to that edition and is reprinted here by permission of the publisher.

with a Southern accent. "Cotta," a white vestment worn in Episcopal choirs, became "carter," and Fayetteville, "Fedville," just as Tennesseans pronounce them. He always wrote "are" for "or." An "unberallow" is used to keep the rain off—or to make metal arrows. Forensic Hall at Sewanee became "Frenzy" Hall—not inappropriate for the site of late dances. We corrected spelling that obscured or distorted the meaning. Ely's spelling suffered as emotion waxed, but his near misses remind us of his colossal accomplishment. I wish I had thought, as did one reviewer, to call him the Grandma Moses of American literature. Scholars can find the original manuscript, in Ely Green's handwriting, at the Jessie Ball duPont Library in Sewanee.

Revealed in this document is something few Southerners have grasped: The aristocrat, protesting he had only love in his heart for the Negro, imposed segregation "for his own good." The poor white became "the law" and in his capacity as policeman, deputy, constable, prison guard, bus driver, railroad conductor, or store clerk enforced the segregation decreed by the white Brahmin. At the point where segregation actually was implemented, the black suffered in proportion to the degree of sadism, malice, hatred, or economic fear which afflicted the red-neck. The tightly insulated aristocrat rarely persecuted the Negro, but the cop who needed somebody to beat could always go into Black Bottom and "whup me a nigger" to gratify his lust. He need fear no reprisal. There were not enough blacks in the South to outweigh the evidence of one white bum before a "jury of peers"—that is, whites. The hapless black fell under the direct control of people who obsessively required someone to be superior to, someone to peck. The aloof aristocrat heard only what he wanted to hear from his confidential advisors—his body servants. And they did not distinguish themselves for loyalty to their own race.

Ely's story is an epic in black history—an epic tragedy transcending nationality. Ely is the Superior Man constricted by imperfect society, by bad laws, by illogical customs. High drama is effected by unbelievable resilience. The folk hero loses a skirmish, revives after near-fatal wounds, and comes back into the war. Always an exile, he is always reapplying for citizenship, always being rejected, always forgiving, and always trying again. Just as no one deserves God's grace, no one deserves Ely's forgiveness, but we cannot help prizing him because he granted it. . . .

What was Ely Green trying to say? What was his message? Improve yourself. Learn from everybody and from every situation. Do not accept the word Negro. It is a slave name. (How tragic that he died in the very year that "black" became a more acceptable term than "Negro," and how strange it is that for so long genteel whites thought "black" a nasty word to call a Negro.)

"It is criminal," said Ely Green, "to call a man who is suppose to be free by the name of a slave, and the world laughing at us about it. There is no race Negro," declared Ely. "I went in World War One into France when I didn't have to go . . . [to prove] that no one can represent America on foreign soil but as an American. . . . I refused on my return to be discharged as a Negro. I have all my life fought for the right of law that is all the black man can ask for. A so-called Negro can't ever have this. To my idea he still represents property. How can he be a citizen?" And he says: "We are going to win our rights in love and peace, if we are going to enjoy it at all." He concludes with majesty: "I am writing this book for both my black and white brother. No prejudice. A book of love."

LaVergne, TN USA
28 June 2010
187669LV00002B/99/A